Sun Mere Bandhu Re

THE MUSICAL WORLD OF S.D. BURMAN

Celebrating
30 Years of Publishing
in India

Praise for *Sun Mere Bandhu Re*

'Really enjoyed it. Good mix of anecdote, analysis, reportage. It took me a long time to finish though, because every mention of a song kept making me go to YouTube and then I'd go to other songs … Addictive stuff.' – Baradwaj Rangan

'The book does succeed in its primary purpose – letting the reader into the mind of the maestro, showing us that beneath SD's celebrated public persona was a vulnerable man who tried to live life by the values he held dear … The book covers significant events in SD's career that highlight his fiercely independent mind.' – Ganesh Anantharaman, *India Today*

'*Sun Mere Bandhu*, much like SD's musical scores, becomes a work to be appreciated.' – Akshay Manwani, *The Indian Express*

'[A] well-researched book replete with anecdotes, instances and occasions one had seldom heard of.' – Ziya Us Salam, *The Hindu*

Sun Mere Bandhu Re

THE MUSICAL WORLD OF S.D. BURMAN

SATHYA SARAN

HarperCollins *Publishers* India

First published in hardback in India by
HarperCollins *Publishers* in 2014

This edition published in paperback in India by
HarperCollins *Publishers* in 2022
4th Floor, Tower A, Building No 10, DLF Cyber City,
DLF Phase II, Gurugram, Haryana – 122002
www.harpercollins.co.in

P-ISBN: 978-93-5629-580-3
E-ISBN: 978-93-5029-850-3

2 4 6 8 10 9 7 5 3 1

Typeset in 12/16 Electra LT Regular at
SÜRYA

Printed and bound at
Thomson Press (India) Ltd.

MIX
Paper
FSC FSC® C010615

This book is produced from independently certified FSC® paper
to ensure responsible forest management.

To my sister Nithya.

Because we grew up singing many of the songs in this book.

Contents

Preface

One thing usually leads to another. The thread of destiny unravels in surprising ways, sometimes telescoping the past and present into a concrete moment.

I have never met S.D. Burman. I know his songs of course, have grown up singing them to myself. I had seen the rare picture of him somewhere, and held the impression of a calm, spartan face that could have been etched in solitude by a calligraphist's pen.

Beyond a chance second-hand encounter with the composer through Abrar Alvi while researching my book on Guru Dutt, I knew nothing about S.D. Burman. And Alvi revealed him only as a gentle soul, possessive about his paan and careful with his money – not much to build an image from.

But one thing led to another. A young man who worked in the same building I used as an office for a while came up to me to say that his father had read my book on Guru Dutt. He wanted to know if I would take on the writing of a biography of S.D. Burman. His father, the young man continued, was a huge fan of the music director, and had collected clippings published about him for the past few decades, which he was willing to hand over to me.

And so it was that I met Moti Lalwani who came bearing his treasure trove. A meeting that resulted in two bulging files in my custody.

This was followed up by a series of interviews that had been conducted for the four fan-page web sites he administered, and an offer to continue to do the interviews of prominent players in S.D. Burman's musical world. Of course, I gratefully accepted.

For almost four months after this, I refused to look at the material on hand. Material that kept coming in, in the form of fresh interviews, and relentlessly stared at me from my inbox everytime I logged on. When I finally began to read, it was like entering a labyrinth. I could so easily be lost in this uncharted territory, where voices spoke from every direction; some echoing, some contradicting one another. Despite so many voices speaking about him, I could find S.D. Burman nowhere. The man was missing.

Adding to my confusion was a package that landed on my table one morning. From Bangladesh. A book on S.D. Burman by a venerable researcher of the composer's work, H.Q. Chowdhury.

My heart sank. Was I heading to a dead end? Was there place for a second book? What could I say that was new about a man I had never met or known?

It was S.D. Burman himself who came to my rescue. His slim autobiographical note, *Sargamer Nikhad*, written with simplicity and a charming lack of self-consciousness was the first real insight into the person I had been looking for. His stories of his youth, his description of his interactions with those who mattered to him in his musical journey through life gave me the clue on how to shape his story.

I put aside everything I had read as notes and interviews. I listened to the songs, I let myself listen to the world around me as someone who heard only the music in every sound.

And the book began to take shape in my mind.

I listened to the music of the birds, to the beat of a butterfly's wings as it flitted past my window. The rat-a-tat of the local train, the shouted cadences of the fruit seller's voice, the spoon hitting the side of the pot in the kitchen … I imagined a musician listening to them and capturing the music inherent in every sound.

And destiny took me back to the days when I walked barefoot in the grass, chasing dragonflies, or lay in the shade of a spreading rain tree watching alternately the clouds or the brown tufts at the ends of the leaves of grass waving in the breeze while far away a man selling mud violins played a tune I knew the words of.

It was easy then to blend the real with the almost real. To let imagination colour the calligraphist's portrait in the shades of music.

By the time this book went into edits, another book on S.D. Burman had come out, this time by an Indian, by someone who shared the surname. But by now I was no longer worried about the content. Another book wasn't going to make a difference because I had decided on a new approach to the narrative altogether.

This narration of S.D. Burman's life follows his journey through it and through his music faithfully. There is nothing in the book that has not been documented elsewhere in print or recorded through interviews for this book. It is only in the telling of the story that I have, like the subject of this book, let myself roam free. Just as he would take the seven notes of music and spin out of them an endless fabric of songs, I have tried to take the many facts and milestones of his life and weave a tapestry that reveals in its intricacies the genius of a man whose life was simply dictated by music.

In doing this, I hope to present S.D. Burman's amazing story not just to those who have been thrilled to listen to his songs, but to a generation that can learn the blessings of a way of life dedicated so passionately to excellence. A passion that never waned, and so touched the hearts of at least two generations of moviegoers.

On learning I was writing this book, a friend asked me why I chose to write on dead people. I replied that I seem to be so chosen. And take it on gladly because I could then try, through my writing, to make them come alive again.

Sathya Saran
April 2014

Amitabh Bachchan
'Prateeksha', 10th North-South Road, JVPD Scheme, Juhu, Mumbai -400 049

6th February, 2013

S.D. BURMAN

His renown came to me much before I met him in person.

An admirer of his music and his unique style of singing, were the greatest attraction.

The sound of his voice was earthy and so drenched with the earth of his land of birth, that it would almost seem that it was not the physical presence or sound of his vocal chords, but the voice and sound of his 'mitti'.

I had been fortunate to have been present on several occasions when he would be recording at sound studios, and to watch him immerse himself in the notes and the tone of the singer, was an exceptional experience. Nothing but the song its tune and its rendition mattered to him when he would record, and the slightest disturbance would be met with strong reprimand.

When Hrishikesh Mukherjee was making 'Abhimaan' with Jaya and myself, we spent a most memorable afternoon at his home where he would sing and render the possible tunes that would form the music of the film. The songs of 'Abhimaan' have been tested through the years and through time without ever seeming outdated or even forgotten. Burman dada gave some of the most melodious songs to our Film Industry, but the music of 'Abhimaan' shall always remain special. We were never able to replicate to its fullest the originals sung by him. They were in a league of their own ...A simple man, with the most simple habits, in the most simplest of environs. His passion was music and it came from his heart!

Amitabh Bachchan

PART ONE

BEGINNINGS

1

He missed being home. The green fields, the chatter of birds, the cries of men hawking their wares.

Here, the very music of life was stilled, and he could not bear the silence. Yet he had no option. This was the way of princes; to learn, to study and grow into fine men who could rule.

And though his father should have been a ruler, but was not; though he himself would possibly never be a king, yet he was a prince.

And so here he was, Sachin Dev Burman, reverentially called Sachin Karta, living among other princes, learning geography and history and math, but also learning somehow to be a prince.

He wondered if knowledge could be thus imparted or princely demeanour thus learned; the masters might know their subjects, but what could they possibly know of how to be a prince? And his mates were an unruly lot: used to getting their own way. Boisterous, pushy and loud, they intimidated the masters. He had little to say to them, or they to him. He was so different, lost in a different world.

At night, when the noise of the school day finally stilled and others slept, he lay awake, his ears straining to hear the music that lay hidden in his mind. The sound of his father expounding on a note, letting a raga unfurl. The flute as it was played in the field nearby, as the farmer sat against a tree, his day's work done, the music soothing his tired limbs. Some nights he could swear he could hear Madhab chanting the singsong shlokas of the Ramayana under his breath as he worked, or singing them out loud in the evenings…

In fact, the music never really went away. Yet one morning when it curled like smoke and played itself out even as the master pointed out hills and mountains on a map on the classroom wall, he put his head down on the desk to fight back the tears.

He longed for the home he knew and loved, where his father would walk beside him across the warm stone floors under the sweeping arches of the palace, singing all the while. Or let him watch while he crafted and shaped, along with the potters, the wet clay to form the idols for worship on puja days. What was his father doing now? he wondered. Was he resting, shaded from the afternoon heat? More likely he was out in the open, along with the gardeners, sliding the trowel into the soft soil, readying it for the plants that he would push into the earth. His home in Comilla. So full of things to do, to see and feel. Not really so far from where he was, but for all he knew, Kumar Boarding in Agartala could be on another planet!

2

Comilla, today, is a bustling town. To get here you need to travel approximately 100 kilometres from Dhaka, the capital of Bangladesh. However, Tripura, in India, is closer, and lies to the east.

Once you leave the town of Comilla and drive into the countryside, the landscape is a kaleidoscope.

Green is a recurrent theme here, the trees arch overhead, fed by the rain that sweeps down for months. The grass glistens like emerald. Every voice has a lilt, like they were born to sing; the fisherman, the shop owner, the man wielding the shrieking machine that sharpens knives ... their voices are different yet tuneful in a strange compelling manner.

Along the village roads, boys and men stand alongside the rain-fed marshes and ponds, fishing for their lunch. Bystanders, dressed in shorts and little else, watch idly, with their arms akimbo. Time is leisurely in these parts, life goes by watched in slow measures.

Drive through the roads, avoiding a mushy pothole here and another there, and wend through green patches and small mossy ponds to the verdant village of Chatra. Wander into the village roads of Chatra where, if you listen closely, you can hear the echoes of history.

Perhaps your footsteps will lead you to the ruin of the palatial haveli that once stood sentinel over Comilla. A place where the clink of chisel against stone punctuated the day as sculptures took shape in a room shaded from the sun. Or where the notes from a raga made patterns of light and shade against the rough-hewn floor of the corridors that ran from one end to the other, connecting rooms once filled with the sound of voices.

Sixty acres surrounded the haveli, and the air that blew through the building was cooled by the water that sometimes lapped against the sides of the large tanks that were on either side of the building. Fish of many colours and sizes swam in them, and if you could peep into history, you would see the young Sachin Karta, prince without a throne, casting his rod into the waters, perhaps trying to still the humming that rose unbidden to his throat, so that the fish would not be disturbed. His skin would be reddened by the sun, and perhaps you would sight his nurse, Robir-ma, come running up, with a cap, or a wet towel to cool the boy's delicate skin that the sun was treating so harshly.

Today the palace lies in ruin. Encroachers have set up camp and the chickens that run around are part of the poultry farm clandestinely set up here. The squawking of hens is the only music that fills the air now. The grass around is dead except during and after the abundant rains that sweep the area along with the rest of Bangladesh. The tanks are choked with dead leaves. The move to create a museum of the memorabilia of Sachin Dev Burman that the government has recently started might bring back some life into the place. Or will it?

A recording of Raag Darbari Kanara, played on the sitar in the dead of night, or a recreation of the prayers and bhajans that Sachin's father Nabadwipchandra recited and sang together with his family every evening, alone can bring us one step closer to resurrecting the dead palace as a living memorial to one of Tripura's most glorious sons.

Press release, 17 January 2012

Bangladesh Prime Minister Sheikh Hasina has promised to convert the ancestral house of legendary music maestro Sachin Dev Burman in Bangladesh into a cultural institute-cum-museum, writers and scholars said here today.

'Hasina assured us that her government would effectively consider our proposal of converting the ancestral house of S.D. Burman at Comilla (Eastern Bangladesh) into a cultural institute cum museum,' said Gautam Das, one of the eight-member team of writers, painters, singers and cultural elite which met her during her visit here last week.

'The house was in a dilapidated condition and some local people had encroached upon it and started a poultry farm in it. After Sheikh Hasina became prime minister, the Tripura Cultural Co-ordination Committee along with a few intellectuals from Bangladesh had drawn her attention to it and steps were taken to protect the house,' Satyabrata Chakraberty, who was also in the delegation said. 'We are hopeful that the Bangladesh prime minister would fulfil our desire as she, in her different speeches here, had mentioned about the affinity between the people on both sides of the border and how Rabindra Nath Tagore and poet Kazi Nazrul Islam had influenced and brought us together.'

3

What is the use of having nine children, Nabadwipchandra Karta thought, as he sat watching the sun set. Indeed, the fading light seemed to symbolize the mood of his life. First the tussle over the right to rule, then the court case, and now this, this supreme loneliness that gnawed like a ferret at him, making him believe that there was nothing but darkness ahead.

He had never been a loser. There was in him the strength to rise again and again from the depths life would lead him to. Depths of despair, of anger, deprivation.

He might have lost his kingdom, he thought, but he had his song. His music and his family were his soldiers in life, helping him conquer new vistas of peace, where the old had been lost.

The blades of grass outside the window moved gently in the breeze. Evening always brought with it this soft stirring of nature's senses. As if on cue, the sun sent a ray of gold to caress the tops of the blades. A blessing to remind him that though it would soon be dark, the light was never far behind.

Sachin would have … the last time they had sat at the same window and watched this very act of blessing, Sachin had said something. What was it, something about … His mind leapt and caught the ferret. Sachin, that was it!

He knew now whence his melancholy rose. The other boys were his darlings too, but they were grown up, and far away in Darjeeling, studying to be men of the world. They would have to take their place among equals and less soon enough and he was glad they were proving fit for the challenge. But this child, this last delicate boy, with a face that reflected every emotion, was close enough, and yet far away. His heart yearned for the child. A man loves his daughters, he thought, but they are women and need the company of their mother more.

A man needs a son by his side.

I cannot be weak, he thought to himself, as he gathered the

folds of his dhoti and rose to move away from the very thought that had presented itself to him. The boy needs discipline, the company of others. He needs to learn many things besides music.

But the thought refused to yield, sitting like a monkey in the corner of his mind, waiting to snatch at his peace.

He woke to the sounds of the night. The chirping cricket, the cry of the night bird hunting … sounds he had heard often enough before.

'What is it?' Nirupama asked, seeing him standing at the window, a brooding silhouette of thought. He shook his head. Undecided. Yet he knew his mind had been made up for him by his heart.

The boy would come home.

4

India lives in song. The oldest stories, the myths, even the epics written in sacred letters by the celestials themselves have been converted to song, set to music and in every little hamlet and craggy mountain village or mud-washed desert town, singers have found voices that sing them in their own tunes. With words adapted to their turn of speech.

The wandering minstrel was both the circus and the saviour. He came through with his bundle of songs, sung in exchange for a smile, a meal or just a glance, and when he had had his say, he would wander off, to sing along his path; the tunes his only company, as he walked the road to his next patch of nowhere.

Perhaps the romance of the road made it happen, perhaps

the haunting voices that drifted in the air as the singing minstrel stepped blithely onward wove itself into his psyche, but when he heard them, the young Sachin could not stay.

Others have been thus captivated by song. Radha left her home without the fear of reproof when the flute played its call by the Jamuna. Whether it was the flute or the player is a matter of perspective, one being as powerful a magnet as the other.

Singers have followed singers; Mohammed Rafi would pad along behind a sage who sang in a voice that moved his childish heart to the core. And Sachin took it upon himself to wander through the muddy paths or squelch through rain-soaked gullies, following the Baul singers who passed through. In their own way, the singer and the follower were seeking their gods.

Art begets art. Pictures turn to words, words to pictures sometimes painted on the walls or on fabric, stone patterns from nature carved on temple walls get woven into cloth, and become symbols in themselves. Music too has its patterns, and Sachin too was exposed to the many layers of music as if they were petals unfurling to the light of dawn. He took them all and held them in his mind, wrapped in a great secret space.

His voice would rise in song; even as a child, he would sing the strains of classical music that he learnt from his father and yet hum the tunes he heard from others, but the composer in him lay dormant. Waiting for the tapestry to be complete, with a pattern all his own. A deft mix of classical and folk, of song and melody, voice and instruments that would be the unique, unquestioned music of S.D. Burman, the composer.

5

A young girl is playing a game of hopscotch. As she hops from one square to another, she hums. As she stops to pick up the stone to throw it, she stops for a moment. Standing there, softly hitting the stone against her chin, lost in the contemplation of where to place it on the squares on the ground in front of her, she sings out the song she has been intermittently humming. The song has an earthy flavour to it. The words are:

Aajke jaabo shashurbari, saajiye de aamay taratari

(I have to go to my father-in-law's house today, dress me up quickly.)

Sachin Dev Burman is watching the tableau. He is captivated by the girl's song.

When the girl's father appears, Sachin asks him, 'What is happening? What are you doing?'

He replies, 'Jo mera ladki hai na, usko shaadi de raha hun.' (She is my daughter. I am marrying her off.)

The girl is very young … so Sachin Dev Burman asks, 'Shaadi de raha hun! Abhi kyon?' (Marrying her off? Why so early?)

Father: 'Bada hoke toh kharab ho jayega. Uski thaali de raha hoon, nahin toh kharaab ho jayega. Abhi dena hai. Usi ka gaana hai, *Aajke jaabo shashurbadi*.' (When she grows up, she might go astray! I am conducting her ceremonies. I have to marry her off now. That's the song, 'Today I am going to in-laws' place.')

♫

From a Khagesh Dev Burman interview by Moti Lalwani and Richa Lakhanpal:

What's more surprising is that the rather jazzy hit song '*Roop tera mastana*' sung by Kishore Kumar is but a beautiful folk melody that SD happened to hear a long time ago. He remembered the tune because of its peculiar effect. It merely uses two notes and has a very special influence on the senses.

6

If he had not lived his childhood in Comilla, maybe the man we know as S.D. Burman might not have become a musician. Or he might have made music of quite a different timbre.

The soil had something to do with it, the sound of water, the rain as it pitter-pattered on the earth hardened by the searing sun. The wind must have whispered to him too, as he walked through the lanes, and the rising and falling voices of those he knew, met or watched from afar. Among them, Madhav and that deft wielder of the do-tara, the open-voiced Bhatiali singer, Anwar.

Madhav was the teller of tales from the Ramayana. The singsong cadences, the deftness of words and the way they were blended into the recitation were obvious influences. As for Anwar, he sang plaintive Bhatiali tunes, strumming the dotara, as he accompanied Karta to the river or sat with him by the lake. They would spend their time fishing, using rods that they had themselves chiselled, an art in which Anwar carefully tutored Sachin. Returning home after a day listening to the boatmen singing their songs as they floated past on their crafts, Anwar would present his own Bhatiali composition to his master. Undoubtedly, Sachin soaked it all in, eager to assimilate every kind of music. Later, the young prince would sing Anwar's songs during his tiffin break as he sat under a banyan tree in the open field.

Little wonder then that Sachin Dev Burman would assert later that though he loved classical music. Madhav and Anwar were clearly his 'first gurus'.

In villages, the boatman turns singer even today. Long hours in the flowing water, alone with the elements, and an ever-changing montage of passengers, give him a view of life different from those who walk on land. The music of the stars above and the moving waters below, the broken rhythms of the fish leaping ahead of the craft he plies, the slap of the oars – all have the ability to ease the voice that might otherwise lie caged within thoughts, and let it flow into song. The deep philosophy of the boatman's songs could not but have an impact on any music lover. Sachin Dev, as he wandered along the Gomti's banks, must have found his ears tuning in to snatches of song, pregnant with layers of meaning.

Sometimes its sound mist him with melancholia; the sight of the boat on the water, the eagles circling high above have an inexplicable effect on him.

♫

It was in Comilla that Sachin Dev's elder brother, Kiran Kumar Dev Burman, himself a gifted singer, shared his love for music with the younger sibling till he joined the army. First by listening and learning and then by singing along or venturing out on his own voice, Sachin Dev let the understanding of classical music enter his soul.

Each form of music carries its own philosophy. Folk songs sing of everyday hopes and aspirations, real and spiritual; bhajans delineate the yearning for the Infinite; classical bandishes have their own layered meanings.

Listening to the words would never make a writer out of the young listener, but the many facets of thought would shape his being, giving him the ability to mellow into a musician who used words as tools to embellish his chosen form of creative expression.

And it was because he lived away from the royal palace – that could well have been his home had fate decreed otherwise – that, through his adolescence and years in college, Sachin Dev was allowed to roam free, following whichever trail of music he could find, wandering through nearby villages to participate at fairs and festivals where rustics and mendicants, fakirs and accomplished trained singers met and sang their own heritage of songs. What a sight he must have made, this thin, fair-skinned young man in a starched white shirt, sleeves rolled exposing knobby elbows; his dhoti marked by the smudges made by the stalks of tall grass that he passed through cutting across a field or running by the river.

Layering on this fertile soil of native folk music in its varied forms was the music Sachin Dev was to be exposed to when his father moved to Agartala to take up position in the royal court as prime minister. Though he continued to live in Comilla, he would often visit his father, spend a few days in the beautiful natural and architectural surroundings of the royal palace.

Here, in the royal court, where scholarly exponents of the classical mode chose to air their talents, Sachin found another source of influence to feed his deepest love.

And an instrument to express the tunes that he found beating against his brain, like so many birds seeking to fly free.

7

Sitting with his legs immersed in the cool water of the Durgabari, he worked on the reed. The knife was sharp, and he needed to be careful, mindful of the flying birds that distracted him with their calls, and the fact that the sun's dazzling rays were sometimes prone to blinding his eyes as they reflected off the water.

This was his idea of bliss; sitting by himself, creating from the unique reeds that grew here in Tripura, an instrument for his tunes. He smiled as he remembered how he had played one night, here, in the moonlight, a string of tunes, one following the other in an unending trail of pure melody. Lost in his own world, he had not realized that the rest of the palace was asleep. And that the music, as it wove its way through the quiet of the night, had entered the room of the sleeping king and his queen and wafted over their slumber, till it woke them. They had opened their eyes to the sound in their ears, and stood by the window listening, till, with sleep calling to him, he had risen and wended his way to his room. He loved the sound of the flute, it was a music with no commas. Unlike the tabla, which he was now adept at, but which was masculine and structured and full of punctuation marks. They were so different, he thought, these two instruments, and yet, they could make harmony together.

Each instrument has a personality, he thought, I need just to understand what it is to get the best out of it.

The sitar and the violin, each capable of drawing tears or making the heart dance, were so different. One, delicate as a maiden splashing in water, the other, a poet sighing in anguish. Yet they were all the voices of his music.

He did not know it then, but they would stay with him all through his life, and he would bring in other instruments to join his familiars: the saxophone, the drums, as well as use non-traditional household things, combs, kettles, to create the sounds he needed to embellish his tune and match it to the scene on screen.

As he mastered the instruments, he trained his voice too, singing the songs he heard, or was taught, preparing the ground, unknowingly perhaps, for the lessons that lay ahead.

♫

Excerpt from S.D. Burman's autobiography Sargamer Nikhad

While I was in standard V, I sang a song taught by my father in a cultural programme during Saraswati Puja in my school. It was 1915 and was my first performance in a public programme. It made me popular among my friends as if I had become a 'Hero'! The headmaster was so pleased that he wrote a letter to my father.

8

Robir-ma: Dulina has not come to eat, where is he? Check it out ayi; see if he is in the back.

Servant: Orey o Robir-ma. You know our Karta. Time has no meaning for him. Sometimes he is at play, sometimes he is humming, or catching fish. Food is not important.

Robir-ma: Stop telling me about my child. Who knows him better than me? I have nursed him with my own milk. Go, go baba, and see if he is at the back, in the tennis court. The racquet is missing, he must be playing there. *(Wipes her face.)* In this heat, eeesh, how can he bear it?

(Man steps out.)

Robir-ma mutters to herself: All the food is cold; the fish never tastes as good when heated again. Where is the boy? *(Looks out.)* Orey, where are you lost now?

(Servant comes in, hurrying.)

Servant: He's gone. His friends are there, but he is not. They say he dropped the match when he heard someone singing in the road beyond, and went after him.

Robir-ma: I have to tell his mother. He does not eat, he is always missing at mealtimes. It will affect his health. Now I am here, when I die who will look after him? *(Shakes her head.)*

Servant: He has so many interests, and all of them are his passions. Football, cricket, tennis, music, tabla, violin ... Baap re, only yesterday, I heard his father scolding him for doing badly in his studies. A prince must study...

Robir-ma: Chup. Anybody can go to school and study, have you heard how he plays the tabla? Or the flute. Like Krishna himself is playing. So sweetly. Anyway, he will soon go to

Kolikata, the big city, there he will have to study. He will study law and become a big vakil.

Servant: Kolikata. Baap re, that is far. Sooo far. But yes, once he goes there he will become a big man, study and become a vakil … but you, how will you live without him?

Robir-ma: I think about it too, and my heart is afraid.

9

Dear Dada,

Pranaam. I am sure you are doing well. I am writing this with mixed feelings.

I wanted so much to be like all of you, study for my BA in Calcutta, learn new things, see the city, but Father is not in favour. He says all his sons are gone far away, and he seldom sees them, and at least I must stay by his side a little longer. 'You are my youngest child; all others are away, so I wish you to be with me at least for two more years,' were his exact words.

Is this a price I must pay for being the youngest? Or is this good fortune?

I know I love Comilla, but there is a wonderful world outside waiting to be explored. I don't want to be a little frog in a well, croaking to myself, I want to explore the city, be in a college with other men like yourself. But it is no use. Father says mother will be heartbroken too, and so, I think that is that. However, I have made him promise to let me go to Calcutta for further studies. Let me see, he said, that is still years away.

When are you next coming, Dada? I wait for your return.

We will have games of tennis and make music together. Do come soon,

Your younger brother,

Sachin.

10

He wonders what his father would say if he saw him now. I could be Anwar's son, he thinks wryly, or of one of these men in whose company I am sitting.

He looks at his hands, the nails dirty with grime, ash from the hookah like dust on his arm. His head spins a little from pulling at the hookah, and then some more when they begin their chanting to Shiva. The voices rise, one overlapping the other, and another. He feels the surge of the wave, pulling him, further and further in.

Oh the sweet power of it. The smoke and the song, and Anwar's voice, calling him, Karta, chalo, Karta, chalo. Chalo. And the tune rising from his head.

Mixed with the songs he had heard, the songs, the chants, he had listened to and learnt. And they swirl in his head … and the tune, not theirs, his, his. He must catch it, hold it, make it his.

The sound of cymbals, the chant, the singer in the distance. But the smoke hurts his eyes and his throat and he cannot soak it all, cannot capture the tune. Karta, chalo, Anwar calling. Let him call.

He lies down, the ashes warm from the fire, Shiva is near, his eye glowing. And comforted, he sleeps.

Much later, when he had no memory of this, the music would weave itself out of his brain, mingled with his breath. He would have by then made it his very own!

PART TWO

CALCUTTA

11

There must be more cows in this city than humans, he thought, looking down on the crowded street. How people jostle and push, and yet nobody notices that there is not enough space for all, let alone for cows!

Calcutta! He had imagined it differently, somehow. The buildings all seemed to be either very grand and stately, or falling apart. The roads were hard, and endless, and there were no trees. No birds sang to him in the mornings; it was the loud raucous call of the crow instead that shattered his ears. And the cries that came floating up in the air from the street as the men called out their wares or their services were shrill and sometimes musical, but very different indeed from the singsong tones he had grown up with.

The nights were his worst time.

His neck aching from poring over his studies in the library, he would step out, and stand at the top of the stairs looking up at the sky.

What sky, he thought miserably, reminded of the first time he had looked to sight his favourite stars, and seen only the blur of ambient light in a sliver of sky.

The city lights rivalled the firmament's, overshadowed it. He missed the quiet of Comilla at night, the moon drifting in the sky, the wisps of cloud lit by the moonlight, and sometimes, the sound of water.

More than everything he missed the river, the sound of the rushing water, the slap-slap of the fish hitting the surface. The sea was far, far away, and the river was beyond his reach.

Nights he would often lie in bed, letting the sounds–the high-pitched ting-ting bell of the tram rattling past to its shed, the occasional lorry horn, the mooing of a sleepy cow calling to another–fade out of earshot, and his mind wander along the river back home.

The sliding moonlight over the water would then enchant him, and he would replay the boatman's song in memory, the spool unwinding slowly till at last he fell asleep, soothed. There was only one solace. In this city of unmusical noise, he had found a guru. He would find his music again.

Soothed by the thought he drifted into sleep, his mind now roaming far away from the hustle of a city where the roads were now full of ruminating cows herded together against the hours till morning.

12

Sitting cross-legged in his characteristic style, he listened, eyes fixed on the singer's face.

Something welled up inside him as he listened, a rushing emotion that engulfed his very soul. There was an unnameable pressure against his chest, as if some gate within would open and send out a flood of feeling.

What does he see as he sings? he wondered. Does sound have an image for someone who cannot not use his eyes to see? His guru was not born blind; he had seen the world around him when he was a boy. How much of what he saw did he remember? How many of those images could his mind still recreate?

Returning one evening from his lesson with Keshto Babu, the blind singer others addressed more formally as K.C. Dey, he had tried to experiment with his day's lesson during his riyaz.

He did his riyaz faithfully, often neglecting his studies when the music elevated him to another plane. His guru mantra was riyaz, it alone was the key to training the voice, to opening the doors to the manifold world of ragas in all their intricate complexities. Faithful to the mantra his guru had given him, he spent hours in his room practising what he had been taught, polishing the notes, and fine-tuning his voice as it articulated the nuances of the lesson.

He had to guard against what Keshto Babu called affectations. The trick with the voice, the tendency to embroider the word, to give it a twist. It was, according to his guru, cheap gimmickry, the sign of a novice trying to impress. The secret of good singing lay in clarity. In a simple exposition of the notes, the clear unfolding of the raga, in a direct and uninhibited use of the voice, and enunciation of the words of the song. Whether it was a classical song or a simple bhajan, the rules were the same. Sing it simple and without excesses. He often recited this to himself before he started his riyaz.

That evening, the thought had struck him, to sing as his guru did, without sight. He had shut the doors and windows, and let the dark enter and take hold of the room as completely as if there was never any hope of light. Then, sitting cross-legged with his tanpura, he had shut his eyes, tying them with his gamchha, to ensure no vestige of light beat accidentally against the closed lids. And he had started his riyaz.

He had never sung like this before. He could feel every note vibrating in his body, swirling through his arteries and coursing through his veins, clear and separate, then welding one into the other to form the raga.

When he finished the session, he untied the blindfold, opened the doors and windows, and let the light in. Through the night he wondered what he had discovered in the dark. And whether the light would take it away.

Now listening to Keshto Babu, he suddenly understood. In every note, in every word, there was that something that shook the heart. Emotion. No wonder the city was mesmerized by K.C. Dey as he sang his own songs in film after film, with directors writing roles for him, despite his blindness.

The emotion was a magnetic force. It was the power of a flood pushing open the sluice gates of feeling in the listener's heart, touching the heart to its very core, forcing him to listen with every fibre of his being. The master gave his music what eyes could not have given it: emotion. He sang with his heart.

That was what caused his own heart to swell with feeling, to yearn to beat in tune with the singer's.

It was a lesson well learnt. He would remember it for all his life.

13

My dear son Sachin,

Your letter distressed your mother and me. To hear that you are no longer interested in your studies hurts me. I had dreams that you would become the most educated of my children, that you would go on to study law and take your place in Comilla where you have duties awaiting you, befitting a prince.

Instead, you are giving up your MA studies. I do understand your love for music, and that you are now learning under the guidance of other gurus too. They are respected names. Khalifa Badal Khan is a venerable singer and a guru of rare talents, he will add to your knowledge, and I am truly proud that he has agreed to teach you. It was indeed noble and gracious of your guru K.C. Dey to allow you to learn from him. Gurus can be very possessive in some instances, but your guru has an open heart and a mind as vast and generous as the open skies.

But I wonder if you could not pursue your studies along with music. How will a prince live by music alone? These thoughts make me worry, and though I do not share them with your mother, I know she has these thoughts too.

I am happy you got your voice back. It must have been very distressing, and if I had known you had lost it, I would have recommended a good doctor in Calcutta who would have helped it come back sooner. So you would have been spared the fortnight of misery.

Please do let us know if you are not in the best of health at any time. It worries your mother thinking you may be hiding illnesses from us, like you did the loss of your voice. The only solace she has is that Robir-ma is there to take care of you. But she is getting old too, and that worries me.

If you have given up tennis as well, on Keshto Babu's advice, and if it was indeed the reason for your voice faltering, please ensure you get enough exercise. You have always been an outdoors person, and the city is constricting, so ensure you take long walks.

I hope you will continue to interact with the friends you made at the YMCA, and keep up with sports. Some of them are good boys who can ease your loneliness in a city far away from home. It is good to interact with boys your own age, frequently in spheres other than music.

Above all, take care.

Your mother tells me to give you her blessings.

Your father.

P.S.: I am coming to Calcutta the day after tomorrow. Please meet me at the Howrah station.

14

Have I failed my son as his father, he thought, as the train rattled on, taking him homeward. The distance between Comilla and Calcutta seemed much longer now, on his return journey, than it had been on his way to the city.

Not quite a fortnight ago, he had travelled there, his mind teeming with thoughts, worry sitting again at his side, a co-passenger. Why do I worry so much about this boy? he had wondered, but worry seemed to be a constant in his love for this one, his most loved, youngest son.

It had been justified, that worry. The nagging feeling that he was losing hold over the boy had not quite proved right, or had it?

He shook his head as if to clear it, and ran his hand over his brow, to ease the frown that in its severity almost gave him a physical pain.

It had all been useless. The arguments he had put forth, the quiet reasonings.

He had gone further, taking Sachin to the college, hoping the imposing edifice with its sanctified air of learning would impress him and change his mind. They had driven past the stately court houses, as part of his ruse to infect his son with a need to belong to the corridors where justice was a living presence, where, as a practitioner of law, after his course in the subject, he would rightfully belong.

Sachin was adamant. Unshakable in his pursuit of his goal. There had been remonstrations, and arguments. Nabadwipchandra sighed as he remembered the long-drawn arguments late into the night.

He would be brilliant as a lawyer. The way he could argue!

The boy was right, he had to grant it to him. Badal Khan was ninety if not more, but in full command of his voice. The boy was lucky to have been accepted by him. He was indeed a wonderful teacher, stricter than any other in his pursuit of perfection. He had made a great impact on Sachin's training. The boy sang beautifully indeed.

Sachin would have made a good lawyer, he thought again, ruefully, recollecting the clarity with which his son had placed before the father his counter arguments. Reason after reason why he would not, could not, return to his books, would not enrol in law college, it was impossible, he said, it would take him away from his pursuit of music, and that was progressing so wonderfully, with his new guru.

I should have sat with him longer through his studies when he was a child, he thought, and less with his singing. Or maybe left him in Agartala in school, where the teachers would have disciplined him better. But I gave in to my need for him to be by my side. It is my fault. How can he ever live by music alone?

O Mother, he murmured through a cloud of despair, help me, help my boy.

He gazed into the distance. The green fields had given way to trees that waved at him in the breeze. He felt a calm smoothing his worry, the breeze through the open window a cool touch against his forehead hot with the thoughts churning within.

Even the lure of going overseas had not tempted the boy, he mused. His passion for music was all encompassing. Obsessive.

But he sang beautifully indeed. Nabadwipchandra took a deep breath and pushed back his shoulders, easing them from the hunch he had been sitting in. What would be would be. Maybe this child of his had his destiny in music. Maybe he would rule the cultural scene in Calcutta one day, holding people captive with his music, just as music held him in thrall now. Maybe all would be well.

He may never become an administrator in Comilla, but at least he was not lost in the city. Moored in his riyaz and his lessons, he was safe from the other dangers the city could pose for a young impressionable man free from the shadow of family control for the first time. As far as he had been able to judge, Sachin had not made acquaintance with any of the vices the city harboured. In that respect at least I have been a good father, he thought. Good breeding can never go wrong.

He watched the changing landscape, and listened to the rat-a-tat of the wheels on the rails. It was so beautiful; the rolling countryside outside his window, the sky dotted with grey clouds that would soon mass together and bring the first showers of cool, fresh rain. The sound of the train, the far-off whistle that rose musically like a flute to end in a shriek, the gentle rocking movement ... He closed his eyes, leaned back and, letting go of worry, hummed a tune.

15

If you know someone who has lived in Agartala, and if they have elderly relatives, an old grandmother perhaps or a grandfather or his brother still alive who can recall things, you can ask them to tell you the story of how Holi was celebrated in that part of the country.

Your narrator will recount then the coming of spring and the celebration that marked the night of the full moon in the month of Phalgun. And the day that follows it.

You will hear then of how the entire city would stop its business of daily living and immerse itself in the festive mood. There would be soirees and groups would troop through the streets, playing the dholak and singing in unison, songs of spring.

Into this scene Sachin Karta would come, like a bird

returning to its nest. He would join in like he had never left the place, never been far away in a city, with city people and their careful ways, so different from the carefree camaraderie of these people.

He would come with a treasure of new songs learnt in the city, tied in the bundle of his throat, and they would throng to him, the young and old, clamouring. 'Sachin Karta, let us listen to your songs, give us the new music, let us sing it together.'

He would share the booty of songs, and together, young and old, men and boys, the thakurs and the kartas, with Sachin Karta the pied piper among them, would wander through the roads, enter the gullies and wind their way through the fields, the drums and dholaks playing, the cymbals chiming to keep the beat, the flute sometimes rising in line with the voices and falling as the voices fell.

Then when the colours were spent and evening came, and the full moon rose on the first night of spring, Sachin would sit among his family and sing to them the new ragas and raginis he had learnt. Explaining to them sometimes what was new in his learning.

Question the familiar some more, and stories will tumble of the visits by the man would win world recognition as the Nobel Laureate, Rabindranath Tagore. Year after year, he would visit Agartala, even visiting the house of Nabadwipchandra at times, and watch the unfurling of the spring festivities.

Did the young Sachin Dev Burman ever meet the Master Poet, you will ask. And the answer would be of course. Many times over. But the influence of the Master on the younger man would come into play only much, much later in his life, in strange and wonderful ways.

16

Fragrance and music have a way of lingering. Faces, names, people get forgotten, but a tune, a vestige of a recital, the melody one heard sung by an unseen voice, can remain locked in memory, to rise unbidden at the strangest moments. No surprise then that a tune not remembered for years, bursts through the gates of the mind, and pushing aside the dreariness of daily living, rises to the lips as a song still ready to be sung or hummed.

Memories of epoch-making performances also have an indelible quality about them. Like legends they grow with telling.

Like these two montages, fixed in the history of Tripura.

The blind singer K.C. Dey singing. Light dances on water with the same ease, a wisp of cloud slips over the moon with similar softness, the clear voice of the bird calling to its mate must have learnt the lilt from the clear notes of this singer. Is no one breathing? Eyes don't blink, lips smile as if they have never done anything else, calm has cast its spell, a calm edged with ecstasy. The songs flow, the words are known to one and all, made famous by plays and moving pictures, yet they are new. When heard live in the voice of the singer, the magic is powerful, and spellbinding, the spell is true and won't be broken.

Even Sachin, their own Sachin Karta, sits entranced, silent

as a statue, humbled by the torrent of music, drenched by its power. He is the student, the supplicant at the fount, hoping to receive what he can. Yet they know, even as he does, that his master knows his worth, knows that some of the legacy of music will pass on to him; to own, to transform, and share when he is ready to share it. And some of the fame and glory too? Perhaps. Who knows.

A few years later, another night, another soirée. The erstwhile young pupil is now the master. The magic is the same, the magician is different. The moon is the same but the light it sheds is changed somewhat as it filters through the ragas that weave through the night. The voice has the same magic, but it is a different voice, shaped by the master, trained by him, in the way it exposes its power and the control over the ragas. But there are layers closer to this soil. There in that lilt of the tune is the boatman's call, here the hint of a baul singer singing to his soul, there the sobbing plaint of the bhatiali. The singer's voice is saturated with them all. And it is from the soul that the voice emerges, as he sings. And the crowd, engrossed, mesmerized blends into him, as one soul, lost in the song.

The son of Tripura will rule as a king someday!

17

He may have known nothing about it, but among the students who learnt from his guru, K.C. Dey, was the master's nephew, Probodh Chandra Dey. Still in shorts and shirt, the boy was fascinated by the timbre of Sachin Burman's voice and his style of singing. Part of learning was listening, imbibing the style, the tune, the undulations of voice and the letting go and pulling back of breath at appropriate points in the singing. And the guru's nephew had the opportunity to listen to many, nay most, of his uncle's pupils. Of all of them it was Sachin he admired most, and whose method made him think that here was someone who indeed had a style of his own and was not a mere mimic of the master.

Little wonder that Probodh Chandra, when he evolved into a singer himself, and was invited to sing at functions in Calcutta, sung songs by Sachin Burman, who by that time had turned composer. And as if returning the compliment, Sachin Burman would in later years find for the young admirer a niche that would place him in the front line of playback singers in the Hindi film industry. A niche that he holds unrivalled even today as Manna Dey.

♫

He used to come home to learn music. Sachin-da was a tennis player and had tremendous attraction to any sport. I was very fond of outdoor games and singing as well. My affinity for sports and his voice is what drew me to him. My uncle's students tended to sing in his style of singing. But Sachin-da created his own unique style. It goes to show what an individualist he was even at that age. Sachin-da was my ideal singer. In college I used to sing Sachin-da's songs.

—Manna Dey in an article in *Star and Style*, 1957.

18

Poochho na kaise maine rain bitai
Ik pal jaise ik yug bita
Yug bite mohe neend na aayi…

—Hindi version of Nazrul's original song '***Arunakanti tabo***'.

♫

Excerpt from S.D. Burman's autobiography Sargamer Nikhad

I had the good luck of knowing Kazi Nazrul Islam well. He loved me a lot and I am an artist blessed by him. I have heard a lot of his compositions: songs and poems. He also liked my songs and tunes. Whenever he came to my house, I used to get enthralled by his songs and poems. Also, when I sang for him in my own style, he encouraged me through his overwhelming admiration. He ordered me to record my songs with his lyrics. I did so and by virtue of Kazi-da's masterly creation, all the songs were very popular. Many have heard my song '*Chokh gelo, chokh gelo, keno dakis re—chokh gelo pakhire*'. The lyrics were of Kazi-da. He had written them within a few minutes for me, with the tune. I had requested him, 'Please write a song for me with some "playful" music like "jhumur", and within minutes he presented me with the song. His association was one of the major incidents of my life.

19

He looked at the note, unfolding it carefully. Ten rupees, a rectangular piece of paper with a king's profile on it, complete with a crown on his head. It promised to pay the bearer the sum of ten rupees. What did that mean in terms one can understand? he wondered. It could mean a new set of clothes, a meal for three perhaps, or it could mean a song that could delight the hearts of others.

That is what it had meant to Nripen Kumar and Rai Chand Boral. Pleased with his song, they had rewarded him with the ten-rupee note.

Ten rupees for ten minutes of singing over the radio. A song that he was told would reach thousands if they were tuned in. The idea of his voice reaching so many pleased him immeasurably. More delightful was the fact that the tunes he had sung were his own, the result of hours of sitting at the feet of the Goddess Saraswati and begging for her blessings as he worked on compositions.

He looked at the note and the single zero seemed to dance and melt and double and triple itself. One lakh, he thought, this ten-rupee note is like one lakh for me. He realized with a start that his eyes were full of tears.

Were they of joy at being recognized as a singer whose voice was worth paying to listen to? He could not tell.

That was the beginning of Sachin Dev Burman's singing career. Trips to the studios for recordings became frequent, almost regular, and though the company he first sang for, India Broadcasting, went bankrupt, the Indian State Broadcasting Corporation continued to call him to sing. The year was 1927 and, even when India gained independence, Sachin continued to be one of the regular voices heard on All India Radio. Along with singing, he had now started composing seriously too.

20

The bell rings. It rings again. I am not getting up, I can't, won't. I want to see nothing, hear nothing. I want to cry, to shout out loud, to bite my lips, or my hand to feel the pain so it will let me forget the pain in my heart. But I cannot bring myself to do it.

Would you have wept, Father, if you saw me as I am now? In this little room with this cot, and this table and two chairs, one a bit rickety. The plate covered on the table reminds me that I have not eaten, that Robir-ma sits in the kitchen, knees drawn, head between them, her cheeks wet with worry and pain.

Would you have scolded me for my independence? Or accepted it as the right thing to do? O Father, music is a wail in my brain, the sitar sobs, the violin weeps, the tabla is a heartbeat stilled. Music makes me cry. It reminds me that you–who alone led me by the hand, who tended to my needs, who taught me the first notes and held me when I fell–are not there any more.

Far away, he is far away, yet near. Somehow always like a flame burning constant in my heart, the warmth of his presence is near, guiding me. My father, my guru of all gurus, my king and teacher, where have you gone?

I want to cry, to bite my lips between my teeth so the pain in my heart can be dulled by the pain of teeth on flesh. I can't bring myself to do it. To do anything. If there is no music, there is no life. And music makes me weep.

How my life has changed. What would you have said, Father, if you saw me now? Would you have accepted the fact that this now is my home? I think you would have. You accepted that music was everything for me. How could I agree to a job at court–numbers and babugiri would have erased the music from my life, as surely as the blotter lifts the wet ink from the page. Only the scars of my dreams would have remained. Yes, I know you would have felt very bad, but you would have agreed this was the only way.

♫

He sleeps. He dreams.

He is running down the sandy bank of the river. The sand tickles his feet, pierces his sole, he looks down to see he is barefoot. Where did I leave my slippers? he wonders.

Placing feet carefully in the footprints on the wet sand, he runs. If he runs fast enough, long enough, if he runs without stopping, without letting the snag in his heart stop him, he will catch up with the footsteps. They will wait for him somewhere. But why are they ahead of him, and not beside him as always? Faster, he runs faster, faster. The river runs slower, the sound of the wind in his ears is like a whistle. The waves crash, crash again. A window bangs. He wakes up. It is dark, and drizzling outside. The sound soothes him, he looks out of the window, and cannot tell if it is tears or the rain that wets his face.

In the dark of the room, a song rises to mind.

It's been a long time. A long, long while. Months.

He lights the lamp, and tears the old pages off the calendar. Tomorrow, he tells himself, will be a day dedicated to music.

Otherwise, everything up to now, his father's teaching, his sacrifices, would be in vain.

21

Safal hogi teri aradhana, kahe ko roye
Banegi asha ek din teri yeh nirasha

Kahe ko roye chahe jo hoye, safal hogi teri aradhana
kahe ko roye…

22

Two milestones mark 1932, the year after his father's death, in the life of Sachin Dev Burman.

The first: his evolution as a teacher of music. Students, who listened to him sing, would patiently try to emulate and capture the quality of his song. Not many succeeded, because his voice and rendering were the sum total of his learning from life and the many teachers, both rustics and ustads, but they found a deeper understanding of music nevertheless. His passion and comprehension of ragas and the intricacies of different styles of singing made him a teacher of rare erudition.

Teaching also helped riyaz. Sachin used the time left from his tuitions to hone his own skills, as he worked with dedication at every aspect of music–from enunciation to voice control, to exposition.

And fate gave him a chance to take his ability to compose further, by placing him as a composer for plays. It was while composing the songs for Sachindranath Sengupta's plays *Sati-tirtha* and *Janani* that Sachin first understood the link between music and theatre, the scene and the singer and the song. It would stay with him for life, breathing realism into the songs he would create for the silver screen.

The second milestone was not as easy to cross. Thirsty now for recognition beyond the periphery he was in, Sachin wished to record his songs. Recorded music was a new craze. HMV was one of the pioneer companies that captured artistes' voices on vinyl.

The story of his rejection by HMV, which incidentally also rejected K.L. Saigal, is an oft-repeated one. HMV turned down both singers because their voices were nasal. Purists did not sing with a twang, they were clear throated and full in voice, and the market would not accept anything less.

Unable to comprehend the rejection, Sachin was shattered. His voice had been praised, his singing style was something the most demanding of gurus had found acceptable and remarkable, but the recording company had made little of all this. Even as they went on to record other folk singers, they were adamant about not giving Sachin his break. Rejection was rejection, the pundits of HMV would not be swayed, and there was no one willing to try to change their point of view.

Competition builds any industry, and risk takers discover diamonds in what others believe is but cut glass. Sachin's despondency changed to hope when, at the behest of friends, he applied to the competitor, wholly Indian owned, Hindustan Musical Products, to be granted an audition.

Rejection stared him in the face once more. The owner was cautious; he was taking on a giant, and an established one at that. And a giant which had in its wisdom rejected Sachin already.

But living on his own, and his infinite faith in himself,

goaded the young aspirant to seek help from well-wishers with influence. A recommendation was sent forth. After some persuasion, more to please his friend than due to any real faith in the singer's potential, the owner of Hindustan Musical Products signed Sachin on.

He would record a song, and would get a royalty too. Though, playing safe, the terms were low; the royalty a mere five per cent.

♫

Excerpt from S.D. Burman's autobiography Sargamer Nikhad

I came to know the renowned film director Sri Madhu Basu. I enjoyed all his productions on stage as well as films. His wife Srimati Sadhana learnt music from me. I sang a song in his film *Selima* in the role of a beggar. It would not be irrelevant if I quote here his version regarding this in his autobiography *Amar Jiban* (*My Life*).

Madhu Basu wrote: 'I rented a flat at Chowringee Place near Roxy Cinema Hall. I brought my family there in early 1933. Sadhana again started learning music. Thereafter, in my flat, music programmes were arranged regularly. Amongst the frequent participants, whom I recall prominently, were Mihirbabu (Sri Miharkiran Bhattacharya, elder brother of Timirbaran), Sachin Dev Burman and Himu (Surasagar Himangshu Datta). I told Sachin about Sadhana's desire to learn music and he was very happy to oblige, obviously, without any remuneration.'

♫

As the tiny gramophone needle scratched its way along the grooves, bringing forth the embedded sound in it, a star was born. It cost one rupee and twelve annas at that time to buy the record with Sachin's voice singing through it–not a great sum by any count. But in his circle, and in the state of Agartala, the prince who had refused to live by royal rules, who had chosen his own defiant path and walked a solitary road, was now a hero! The magic of his understanding of all sorts of tunes, the blending of classical and rural airs, the pain in his voice that soared high like a kite or dove deep into the lower octaves like a kingfisher diving for fish had by turn startled, delighted, mesmerized listeners. Hindustan Musical Products had a new musical star! Not surprisingly, other breakthroughs in music followed. K.L. Saigal was among those who were signed on by the company. The era of new voices was opening its eyes.

More milestones were to follow, more records, each more popular than the last; some are still played in many parts of Bengal. The next three years saw his rise as a composer–singer, carving his own niche in the world of music, creating songs for the Puja season. His prowess as a classical singer was matched by his ability to imbibe and translate the nuances of the folk music of various parts of India in his songs. Yet he thirsted for a wider audience than what the radio and the vinyl could give him. Luck, which had smiled on him through the early forays into the public arena of music, held back again. His first recording for film was scrapped and resung by Pankaj Mullick. If he was disheartened, as he must have been, struggling to make his name and find his place in the sun, in a milieu not approved of by his family, Sachin did not let it stop him. He knocked on Dame Luck's door till at last she relented.

Songs for movies followed, he could compose and sing a number or two, and their instant success ensured him more assignments. Invitations to perform at classical soirees, at the Classical Music Conference in Allahabad, led him to meet stalwart singers and interact with them, creating bonds that would span their lifetimes. Life began to show promise in other ways. The one-room tenement was abandoned for a bigger house, and the small group of students who had gathered to learn swelled to more formidable numbers. Among them was one who would walk in step with his music for the rest of his life.

23

Many years later, while setting a song for Bimal Roy's *Sujata*, S.D. Burman was to query the director who demurred at the idea of a song sung by Sunil Dutt over the telephone to express his love for Nutan.

'Have you never been in love?' he is reported to have asked. And pushing aside Bimal Roy's doubts, had gone on to compose the song that would make cinematic history as one of his best, most romantic compositions.

Jalte hain jiske liye teri aakhon ke diye,
Dhoond laya hoon wahi geet main tere liye...

♫

He lies awake. Outside the window the stars twinkle conspiratorially. They have guessed why he, who normally sleeps the sleep of the innocent, is staring at them through the long hours from night to predawn. His sleep has been fitful for nights in a row; his mind by day is buffeted as strongly by thoughts as the water in the river is when the wind rises and pushes the waves to the shore.

I am caught in a tempest, he thinks, and wonders how he will resolve it. He knows there is only one way. The right way. And he sees that taking it will mean happiness. There is music and there is love, he thinks, and together they will blend into a sweet life ahead.

Our voices match so beautifully, he muses. When we sang that duet at the Allahabad Music Conference, it was like nothing I had ever sung before. And the applause – I can still hear it, like rumbling thunder.

Like I remember the way she looked at me when the clapping began, he thinks, a look so sweet, so full of expression. The thought of that expression – it makes him sit up, bolt upright.

That look, he wonders, for the hundredth time, what did it mean? That look…

Was it joy? Or gratitude? A student thanking her teacher for giving her the status of an equal? Or could it be something more? He walks, paces, and looks out into the dark. Above his head, the stars twinkle.

She would be right for me, I need a companion, a friend and fellow lover of music, he thinks. And she has it all. She had learnt classical music under Sri Bhishmadev Chatterjee and dance under Srimati Amita Sen, youngest daughter of Pandit Kshitimohan Sen. Later, she received training in thumri and kirtan from Sri Dhirendrachandra Mitra, and in Rabindrasangeet from Sri Anadi Dastidar.

She will be the right person. Someone who can blend her voice with mine.

He knew she was skilled. The months of her learning from him had told him that. She was well learned too, and well brought up in a genteel home. Her father a judge of no mean standing in the community. Ah they had taught her eyes to speak, those dance lessons! But who would teach him to unravel what they said?

He sighs, and picks up his flute. Music might provide him respite, if not an answer.

24

Tere mere milan ki yeh raina,
Naya koi gul khilayegi...
Tabhi to chanchal hain tere naina
Dekho na
Dekho na, tere mere milan ki ye raina

♫

Respected Mother,

Pranaam. No, I am no longer angry. I believe anger is a wasteful emotion. It corrodes the mind it lives in, and gnaws silently at the heart that gives it room.

I just made a resolve and have stuck to it. To me it has never mattered; the accident of being born rich or poor, royal or commoner. And you know that too and have accepted it. Your presence at my wedding and boudi's presence told me that your love for me was an acceptance of Meera and my choice of her as a wife.

But the visit to Agartala is something that I will never forget. And will never repeat. I never wish to remember or relive it in memory. The agony of rejection is too sharp a pain.

I think royalty is about being large of heart, open of mind, generous of spirit. But our relatives proved to be more miserly of heart than the poorest in the land. They treated Meera worse than they would a servant who wanders into their private chambers. She was brave of spirit and bore it all well, but it is my responsibility to ensure she is never hurt that way again.

I vowed to take care of her and provide for her, and I mean to do both for the rest of my life.

Please don't ask me to visit the palace again. Nothing will change. And I don't care if it does. We have each other and our music. And by God's grace we are doing well. My life has now taken a new turn, and I seek your blessings as we walk this new path, Meera and I.

And I seek your blessings again, for what is to come. Just today, we have been told that we will be parents when the year turns towards a new one. You will be grandmother once more. If father was alive, he would have sung all evening in joy, I know.

Fondly,
Your son,
Sachin

25

1939. A milestone year in the life of the man we all know as S.D. Burman. He did not know it then, but he was one step closer to claiming immortality in the world of music. Not just with his own compositions and his voice but with those of the son who was still a squalling babe-in-arms. A son born to parents with deep-rooted musical talents who would in his time blaze as bright a trail as his father's; and in some ways surpass him in popularity by becoming a symbol of the new and adventurous for the younger generation.

True to his grain, the son, though named Rahul, would be called by a pet name derived from music: Pancham. The fifth note of the musical octave holds the seven notes in perfect balance. Ironically, Pancham would use that very balance to turn music on its head and create new harmonies that were till then considered impossible!

Songs continued to pour out of Sachin Dev Burman through the year, garnering for him unprecedented local success. His ability to blend the classical with emotion, and add a contemporary touch to the old, known ragas set his compositions apart, opening listeners' hearts to new responses to a music they were familiar with. It should have pleased the composer, this success. But something gnawed at his mind; the need to cross the physical boundaries that held his talent; to go beyond, to take the great leap into the rest of the country and stun them with the scope of his music. Even composing for Bengali films was not quite fulfilling. There had to be some way to get out of the walls of the narrow well that surrounded him.

Even as he strained to find his future, Sachin seemed to wish to hold on to his past. In a tribute to his father, Nabadwipchandra, he published a musical booklet. Titled '*Surer Likhon*', each of its pages contained the words and notations of one of Sachin's songs, numbering twenty-five in all.

Incidentally, if a copy of this now extinct volume is found in some forgotten trunk in some music-loving family's attic, it should be a priceless treasure, worthy of being a museum exhibit in Comilla!

26

What is left here, he thought. This city I have grown to love, has betrayed me. I am like the moth beating its wings inside the glass funnel of a lamp; unable to get out, unable to fly. It taunts me with intimations of fame, or success, then hides it all like a capricious elder teasing a child. And now this!

O Calcutta, I have hated you, I have loved you, I have made you mine. But you have robbed me of my peace. Ever since I came here, the blows on my mind have been constant. First my father gone, and I know you robbed me of my remaining years with him with your temptations. And now you tell me my brother is gone. To where he will sing to me no more, to where I can never hear his voice again. My brother, my dear brother, lost to me first when he joined the army, yet close to my heart, our hearts entwined in a unique bond. Now gone from me forever.

I thought my heart could take no more pain. But it swells with every breath and fills me with unbearable anguish. Even the sight of my Pancham, toddling around on fat legs, his chubby fingers playing with the keys of the harmonium, does not ease the pain I feel. One after another you take my dear ones away. My friend, my poet, my inspiration, you have robbed him too!

Ajoy, my childhood friend, why have you left us bereft? How could you go away leaving the music we created, you, Himangshu and me, breaking the tryst we had made as the 'Comilla trio' to put our town on the musicial map? Your voice, the songs you wrote for me, haunt me. When I hear your song '*Aalo chhaya dola*' playing anywhere, it brings tears to my eyes. I cannot bear it. What a team we were. And now … The songs are all I have left to remind me of a friendship that was forged out of music.

Calcutta, I do hate you. I shall desert you as you have me, and find solace in some other place. Find new songs, new vistas. And try to ease the pain that just won't go away.

You have wounded me, Calcutta. Though I loved you and made you my own.

Yet, if I leave you, where will I go? Where do I belong? How can I go far away from my home? Where my life flows in harmony with nature…

♫

On the music front too it seemed that he had come against a wall.

A strange wall that offered no opportunity, no chance.

It was not that he had no influential friends. He was surrounded by them – producers, singers, directors in Bengali cinema. They knew his talent, knew his mastery of the song, he had travelled with Saigal and Pahari Sanyal, he had played tennis with P.C. Barua of New Theatres.

He remembered wryly the time he had followed Saigal

on stage at a concert, and the audience had not turned him down as lesser than the great singer, but listened in rapture. In fact, Saigal, though rushing away for his next appointment, had lingered, entranced by the voice and its unique timbre and the rendering of a song, '*Ami chhinu eka*', that was in the same metre as '*Kaun bujaye Rama, tapat more mann ki*' that the singer himself had recorded not so long ago.

But it had all come to naught. His attempts at finding a foothold as music director had all come up against a wall. A wall so smooth he could not scale it, a wall that offered no explanation.

It was not for the want of trying. He had put aside his pride, had indeed in most unprincely manner walked the hard path of asking for work, traversing the road from one studio to the other.

In his heart of hearts he knew he alone was the cause of his not finding his goal. His tunes were complex. The voices and styles of the singers in films were trained differently, and could not rise to the level of experimentation his tunes demanded of them. And directors either ended up asking him to sing his own compositions and therefore having to give him a role in the film, or turned away the idea of employing him as music director.

Those who did give him a chance would avoid him the next time. His music, though beautiful in composition, failed to create magic on screen. The songs, sung in other voices, failed, dropping like stones in slush, with one single distinct plop.

I should be happy with my successes as a singer, he told himself often. Every record of his, every song he composed and sang was a record of popularity. His father would have been so proud! But his mind would not be satisfied. Like a child crying for the moon, it yearned to see his name as music director in an unending list of films.

It was never going to happen. The salt of success would never tickle his tongue. He knew it.

He had heeded one call to leave Calcutta and venture into the wider film world in Bombay. A brief adventure, not entirely pleasant. It was a strange city with different ways, the people so apart from one another, so different from those he knew.

He had spent days in Bombay a few years ago when they had called him to sing a song for the film *Taj Mahal*.

He could still taste the sea air, the saltiness of it covering his face with a strange mist. The damp of his cotton kurta in the heat; he remembered it all very well. And the strange ways in which they spoke to each other. The studios, the clash of languages, Hindi, Bengali, Marathi–all coming in snatches. It was a strange world indeed, and he had been quite happy to come back. And refused the offer that came a year later to join a studio as composer.

He frowned, wondering if he had done right in turning down the chance.

Yes, he would take the next opportunity. He would go. Leaving all this behind. The bitterness of his failures, the scent of his successes, the well-worn roads, Calcutta, Agartala, he would leave it all. Fly into the sky like a bird released from a cage and test his wings in the new, open space.

But … he wavered. Would it mean losing the old life forever?

The thought of never seeing Agartala again hurt him, but

it would be a distinct possibility if he did indeed take up the call to move to Bombay.

Agartala! A part of him still belonged there, the long walks in the fields, the moonlit nights laced with music, the flute song rising like smoke in the misty evening … the memories were sharp as a knife, plunging into his consciousness. How could he lose touch with his roots?

From Calcutta he could still go home when he chose, a journey not so far, and quickly traversed. Cutting the distance between the present and the past in one swift train ride, blending his present with his childhood.

Is it my destiny calling? he wondered. Does it want me to wander in new fields, find new ways?

Should I follow the call, as I did earlier, when I came here to this city?

He could not guess the answer to that question. Sighing, he sat down, cross-legged as was his habit, folding his dhoti neatly between his legs. Perhaps a song would ease his sorrow and clear the confusion crowding his mind. Drawing the harmonium closer, he closed his eyes and began to sing. He did not notice his son coming closer and sitting by him, listening quietly, eyes wide, head cocked to the sound.

From the room beyond, Meera heard, and drawing closer watched the scene. The frown that furrowed her brow eased as she listened. She sighed. As long as Karta had his music, all would be well with her world.

PART THREE

BOMBAY

27

The sunset here is beautiful. The sea awaits the sun like a mother waiting to cradle the head of her child in her lap. And the sun, like a wilful child, plays his games. Sometimes he hides behind a cloud, he changes colour, hiding behind curtains of pink, blue, purple; he stretches his arms and reaches into the sky as if he could climb back to the heavens.

I love the sunset; it helps me forget the beauty of the sunrise that I so miss in this city.

The sun was my companion in my morning walks. Here too I walk every morning. Keeping in mind what Father told me about always being energetic. But the sun is not by my side, rising slowly along, measuring my pace, smiling softly with half-open eyes at my exertions. I miss the waking sun. But I know that in the evening, I will see him readying to sleep. I must get used to it.

As I must get used to the sea. And make it sing to me the songs the Ganga sang, as her waves lapped the shore in the breeze.

Maybe if I had realized this city had no Ganga, and that I would miss it so much, I would never have come. But here I am, and it is done. And I must learn not to live in the past. At least I have my music. And once I get some good assignments, I can always go back.

♫

Excerpt from S.D. Burman's autobiography Sargamer Nikhad

I found Bombay a city engaged in cultural activities, busier and more cosmopolitan than Calcutta. Famous singer Sri Pannalal Ghosh, music director Sri Anil Biswas, actor Sri Pahari Sanyal, sound recordist Sri Robin Chatterjee–I met them all again in Bombay. But somehow, I felt at the beginning that without the Ganga, without leisure, there was no rhythm to life. I felt very isolated. I was a little depressed, missing my intellectual friends and the atmosphere of Calcutta.

28

Dear Meera,

I hope you are happy in Calcutta with our son. I think he will study well and be no trouble for his mother, at least I hope so. Here, without you, I am lonely. Like a boat adrift. This city gives me no moorings. Work is steady, I sit with my music through the day, and often in the night, it is never away from me, as you well know. But yet, what a strange place I have brought myself to!

You will laugh if you see me at work. Like a caged bird. I am forced to sit in a small room, with 'music director' written on the door outside. It is in line with other such rooms, and sounds emerge from these too as I walk past–of voices, of shouting as tempers rise, of laughter, and sometimes of music.

I am not the only music director in the studio. At Filmistan, there is also Khemchand Prakash babu. You know I have met him in Calcutta, he used to be Timir Baran's assistant then. Today he is a composer for this studio.

All roads seem to lead to Bombay, your Karta too, seeking to infuse his music with the freedom of wide open fields and the melody of flowing rivers, has walked the same road, to end up in a small room!

But no matter. When I close my eyes I can see everything I want, the river, the sky and the green fields, and the tunes flow.

Oh, and I must say, I now have friends, and they speak Hindi better than my broken words. They have helped me make my writer partner, that man named Nepali, understand what I want in lyrics, so he can articulate words to match my tunes. What a long-drawn process!

Do you remember how Nazrul wrote '*Kuhu kuhu koelia*' in five minutes? What a moment it was of brotherhood in creativity and music!

One minute, Nazrul was struggling with the tune, and listening to the koel. I wandered in, still lost in the Khambaj I had just heard Ustad Faiyaz Khan sing. And Nazrul made me say kuhu kuhu, which of course I did, infected by the raga in my mind. The song wrote itself. So simply, like a stream flowing from a glacier, a flower falling to the ground.

But why am I telling you this? You already know the story and the success of the song!

But now, this long-winded method. Meera, I want to come back, sometimes I feel I will simply walk out of here, pick up my suitcase and come back. But my destiny keeps me tied.

You will see, your Karta will surmount this too, for his music.

Tomorrow I will record the first song. The film is called *Shikari*. I am hoping that I won't be the shikar. Ha, I can even joke! I am happy, and nervous. I wish you were with me. But then again, I know you are.

My love to you and to Tublu.

Sachin

29

Sachin had a foothold in the world of Hindi film music now. Filmistan was a friendly place, people were always ready to help the austere-looking, thin, dhoti-clad man who spoke in a funny Bangla accent and kept a lot to himself. He was respected because of his dedication to music, to his work. In fact, his struggles with Hindi and with the conducting of the orchestra during rehearsals and recordings were so obvious that offers of help came on their own.

One such offer came from C. Ramchandra, till recently an assistant himself, now, like Sachin Dev Burman, a music director seeking his own space. Perhaps C. Ramchandra realized that helping another person struggling like him would only help him grow as a human being.

The music scene was crowded with names of considerable popularity; names with diverse approaches to music, all of whom had found their own niche and fans. Madan Mohan, the redoubtable Naushad Ali, Anil Biswas who towered over them all with his sweet melodies, O.P. Nayyar who looked like a foreigner and made music that had the beat of foreign hearts, Shankar and Jaikishan, maestros in making every kind of music from the melodious to the invigorating ... the firmament was crowded with stars on the rise. And here were new claimants for space!

They would do well to help each other, so the young Maharashtrian must have thought, as he took upon himself the onus of recording the songs for *Shikari*. The composer of the music, Burman dada as CR called him, sat quietly as he watched and listened. Learning the strange new ways of the world that was soon to be his own.

But even as he adapted to the ways of Bombay, Sachin Dev Burman found his heart still living in Calcutta.

His family lived there, a strong magnet of course. He longed to see his son. But Bombay was no place for a child to grow up in; he needed the nurture of his own culture, his own people. Then there was the music of his Bengal, the soft-flowing notes, the heart-tugging tunes. He created them as he wished, letting the music flow, when he went back every winter. Unlike in Bombay, where the dictates of public taste, screen situation and the producer's whims steered his songs.

Ah winter! What a time it was. Meera would cook the fresh winter vegetables he got from the market, picking them himself, as he delicately made his way through the narrow rows of sellers, ensuring his dhoti remained spotless even as he skirted past cycle tyres and damp-edged wicker baskets. The fish was fresh too, and perfectly seasoned. His eyes would gleam with joy as he sat cross-legged to eat, his son beside him, watching him take the food to his mouth, mimicking his actions.

His songs would float in the air during the festive season, and his heart would dance with an inexplicable joy hearing the tunes, catching the words in his own powerfully sonorous voice. This was his life, his home. This alone was his music.

Or was it?

At night, as he slept, the thought crawled back into his mind and, pushing away the elation that dwelt there, whispered to him that he had to leave soon, to go back. His destiny awaited him in Bombay.

30

Bhulaye amay dudin / sheshe ki hai bhulbe …

How did I know that I was writing the song for him? I wove the tune to fit the words, because they were beautiful. Sad soft words, redolent with sorrow and memories. Not my memories, then, but of the poet. I wondered what he might be lamenting, the passing of a love, of an era, of a moment?

Now it is I who lament.

I did not imagine I would be back in Agartala so soon. But Prafulla-da is gone, to be with father and brother. I am left behind. To sing in his memory, to keep going when they have stopped. My path is long, and lonely. But I must go on.

Life flows by, I feel I am in a dream, drifting like a boat in the water, the oars lost somewhere, the boatman asleep under the open sky, unmindful of where he is being taken.

I am walking now, through a fair. It symbolizes to me the many aspects of life, the noise, the colour, the Ferris wheel rolling up and down, children screaming, adults looking scared as the box tumbles as if free of its moorings.

They are singing songs of praise outside the dargah, open-throated, full of passion, but I sense the quiet of the man beneath the earth. Does he hear? Does he sense the piety, the reverence of those above? Can he smell the incense? It rises upwards while he lies deep below.

Why am I here? Seeking peace? When death whispers so close, one seeks peace everywhere one thinks it can be found. And a saint is a source of quiet, of peace. But the noise around...

I must keep going.

Yes, for the sake of those who wait for me at home. I must.

I shall return to my song. My music. I have that to look forward to. Meera and I will sing together this year. *'Aj dol dila ke'* – the song is ready, waiting. We shall sing it, like old times.

For Meera, I must shake this melancholy off and be myself. I must be good.

♫

Excerpt from S.D. Burman's autobiography Sargamer Nikhad

Meera, besides composing lyrics, was knowledgeable in creating music too. With her help and assistance, I successfully composed music for many songs, which subsequently became popular. She wrote the mukhras for a number of my popular songs. On many occasions, Meera would write the Bengali lyrics according to the rhythm and metre of my music, making it easier for Hindi lyricists to write their lyrics. I recorded six songs written by Meera for HMV. My life partner Meera – her help, support, encouragement, motivation and sacrifice – has played and will always play a vital role in the success of my musical career. I think of myself as very lucky in having a person like Meera as my wife.

31

Excerpt from 'The Road to Success' by Sachin Dev Burman (Filmfare, *1955*)

'You enter a garden house with a beautiful garden and congratulate the gardener. What about the master of the house?' thus said Shri Ramakrishna. In our film world the same question is often asked, though in different words.

However, let me assure you that as a director of film music, I do not envy the film stars or the playback singers, except when I am called a 'bundle' (a word of unknown origin heard in Bombay which means a good-for-nothing fellow).

One day I had some business at Kardar studio. A fairly big crowd was waiting at the gates for a glimpse of the stars and I drove in, in my car. 'Who is it?' they anxiously asked and peeped in. 'Oh!' came the loud voice of a disappointed fan, and then, 'Arre, he is a bundle.'

But I have my admirers, too. Once I was waiting at the Bandra station to catch a train for Malad. Suddenly, I discovered that the train had come, halted and left. What was I doing? Well, I was lost in the enjoyment of my own tune of a song from *Shabnam* which a gang of labourers were singing to the rhythm of the movements of their hammers and shovels.

Talking of rhythm, I am tempted to repeat an old story. I had just joined Filmistan and at an informal gathering at Malad I was giving a recital of my songs before S. Mukherjee, the Filmistan Chief, Ashok Kumar (Dadamoni to all of us), Pradeep, the lyric poet, and others. In the midst of it I heard a jarring sound which was supposed to be a message of appreciation from an admiring listener. Who could it be?

I looked in the direction of the sound and turned pale. The culprit was none other than my boss, Mr Mukherjee, whom I knew to be a true lover of music and whose style of singing was like my own. How could I satisfy his ears?

As days went by, I made further discoveries regarding his sense of rhythm and harmony. Every day after lunch I had to carry my harmonium to his room. Lying comfortably on a sofa, he listened to my compositions, then closed his eyes, and snored! The snore implied that my composition was disapproved.

This ordeal continued for nearly two months and I came to the end of my patience. I also came to the conclusion that if I could not please my boss, there was no point in my staying on at Filmistan, just to sing lullabies to him. The next day I went prepared for a showdown.

As usual I started playing the harmonium and went on humming my new tune till my boss's eyes closed. There was nothing more to do. I had only to wait for the inevitable snore. But suddenly the boss woke up and said, 'Mr Burman, why don't you get it recorded?'

'Record what?' I asked

'I mean this tune. You may call the musicians and start rehearsing right now,' he said.

I was puzzled and wondered why of all the tunes I had composed for him he liked this one. I found out the same evening. As I was coming out of the rehearsal room, the 'room-boy' (doorkeeper) was humming the tune and quite correctly too! This gave me an idea. From that day I made it a point to get my tunes 'approved' by the 'room boy'. It worked. In almost all cases the room-boy's approval carried.

The secret of Mr Mukherjee's judgement was, as he told me one day, the formula of universal appeal. He said, 'You see, Mr Burman, you have your own style of music, which I like. By all means keep it up but present it in such a way that film lovers may like it and feel at home with it – not only in Bombay or Bengal but all over the country.'

With this and many other pieces of sound advice the man who had apparently no rhythm or harmony guided me over the difficult road to success for which I shall always remain grateful to him.

It is not the composition of music alone that makes a 'hit' song. One is on tenterhooks for fear that a thousand and one calamities may spoil the song. For instance, imagine everything set ready for the final 'take' but the singer nonchalantly enjoys ice chips before singing an important song. And who could it be but Dadamoni? The idol of the Indian screen was to sing a song in *Shikari* and he had been ordered that he should have ice before singing my song to improve his voice! But, believe it or not, to my great amazement and unbounded relief, Dadamoni's voice did improve and became more and more steady as lumps of ice went down his throat.

I cannot explain the medical theory, but I would like to tell my friends, the playback singers who sing my songs: 'For heaven's sake, don't ever try Dadamoni's trick on me. I am already a "bundle" – of nerves!'

32

Everywhere he goes, the song follows. Like a faithful dog seeking a new master.

I wonder if it is telling me something. '*Jab tumhi chale pardes, lagakar thes*'.

I am in pardes, after all.

It's a sweet tune. I find it winding into my mind, unbeckoned.

I am a full-fledged director of music now. Everyone acknowledges that. Pradeep's poem, '*Dol rahi hai naiyya*', set to my music is well liked. The reviews are good, some of the papers have praised the lyrics, the song, and also Dadamoni's singing. All that ice did not hurt–how scared I was when he crunched cubes of ice before the recording! It still amazes me. I wonder what his throat is made of.

My tunes with G.S. Nepali's lyrics are also getting a pretty good response. I should be happy. But am I?

Am I turning into a bitter, unhappy, grasping person? Is it because I live alone? Meera would rebuke me if she were here, this constant need that chips at my mind, shaping thoughts that are otherwise alien to me.

What is success? Is it having plenty of money? Is it finding favour? Then I have both. I am comfortable now, I have found favour with many who have heard the songs of *Shikari* and liked them. Then what is it I seek?

Is it the approval, the roar of the crowd that I want to hear? Even that was not enough in Calcutta, where I got praise from every quarter. Is it the need to surpass all others, then, that nags me? I stop there. I think. I hold the thought like a crystal and turn it this way and that.

Yes, that is it. The song that follows me is the thing.

If '*Dol rahi hai naiyya*' is so, so good, as the writers in the papers are saying, why is even my servant singing '*Jab tumhi chale pardes, lagakar thes*'? Why is it not my song he hums?

No, it is not happiness I seek, or success. It is the magic I have lost. Of touching the heart. Of creating a song that reaches out and wraps itself around every heart it encounters. Till it ends up finding its way into their minds, and on to their lips.

Bombay has made me self-conscious. I must put aside my pretensions and become a villager once more. Seek the roots that nourish my music.

I have solved the problem. Relief!

And now I have a new guru. A helper who cleans my room. I composed a tune that Shashadhar Mukherjee liked. And when I was preparing to record it, I heard the servant boy humming it.

Meera, if you had been here, I would have come dancing home to tell you that I have at last succeeded. Made a tune that lifts the heart of everyone who hears it, and which can stay in the mind easily for a long time. Which anyone can make his own. It is true happiness. I have found it.

Is it not surprising, the lessons life teaches? That anyone can be a guru, if one looks carefully, one can learn from the smallest creature lessons of great value.

33

Sachin Dev Burman had arrived at last. His songs for *Shikari* and *Eight Days* had been well received. His reputation as a sincere musician who sang as beautifully as he worked hard on his tunes gave him a credibility that drew singers to him. By his second film, *Aath Din*, Dada, as he was now being addressed, had also learnt how to manage his own orchestra. He would, as he went along, evolve his own method of working with his musicians, using them sparingly, to add to and not overpower the simplicity of his melodies.

History records the fact that the songs of *Aath Din* were notable for two reasons.

One, for the first time, Kishore Kumar sang for films. The song: '*Banka sipahiya, banka sipahiya*'. He was part of the chorus.

♫

Excerpt from Kishore Kumar's interview by Ameen Sayani (permission to reproduce courtesy Moti Lalwani)

Sachin-da made me sing my first song in the film *Aath Din* – it was not a complete song, just two or three lines. My first complete song for him was in the film *Bahar*. The song was '*Qusoor aapka, huzoor aap ka, mera naam leejiye, na mere baap ka*'. This song was, however, not recorded in Bombay, but in Madras. He put me up in his own room there. And that is when I understood that music was his entire life. Whether he sat or stood, walked or roamed around, music would be with him at all times. Everything he did was musical, sureela. Sachin-da would repeatedly teach me, ai Kishore sing this, sing it like this, sing it with expression, don't embellish it too much, don't try gimmickry, they don't really make a difference, sing it straight and the public will enjoy it all the more. Understood?

♫

Speaking of Kishore Kumar and why he encouraged him to sing, S.D. Burman says in an interview in Marathi to *Rasrang* magazine in their Diwali special issue of 1966 (translated by that author):

> I was very impressed by the quality of Kishore's voice. Which is why, despite the producer's opposition, I insisted he sing in *Aath Din*. Kishore was not a known singer then. But I felt his songs should find favour, and so repeatedly gave him opportunities to sing. After *Aath Din*, I took him for *Bahar* deliberately. He used all the opportunities I gave him with sincerity. He used to copy Saigal at first, as Saigal was his idol. I told him, rather challenged him, to find his voice. If he wished to get ahead and shine, he must stop copying, I told him. He understood and started singing in his own voice. But when he had to sing a sad or meaningful number, he would sing in Saigal's style, or at least one could see the influence clearly.

♫

Excerpt from S.D. Burman's autobiography Sargamer Nikhad

I also discovered Kishore Kumar, the youngest brother of the famous actor Ashok Kumar, as a singer and gave him the opportunity to sing for Hindi films. I was then working at Filmistan in Dadamoni's own production, *Eight Days* (1946). After his matriculation examination, Kishore used to come down to the film studio. Dadamoni once requested me to hear Kishore sing. Kishore had no formal training and never practised, but his natural god-gifted voice enthralled me. I used

Kishore for a song in the same film. The first 'take' was 'okay'. Thereafter, I told Dadamoni that there was no need for Kishore to go to college for conventional education; instead, he should opt for a career in music. After that Kishore firmly established himself as a playback singer in Hindi movies.

♫

And the second reason *Aath Din* is notable for is the fact that it also introduced the voice of Meena Kapoor, who was to later become Anil Biswas's wife.

Meena Kapoor clarified in an interview that her first song was actually for a film called *Pul*, but *Aath Din* released first and thus became the vehicle for her debut.

Hailing from a royal family, Meena Kapoor had often encountered the music director at family events in her childhood. Meena had listened to his records in Bengali as she was growing up, and admired his music.

In getting Meena Kapoor to sing for films, S.D. Burman would carve a path he would take whenever he spotted talent.

Meena Kapoor reports that Burman Dada was well acquainted with her father, the New Theatres actor, Bikram Kapoor. Here, culled from her interview published by the S.D. Centenary Committee in its exhaustive and informative souvenir, is an excerpt in Meena's own words:

> **How did you end up singing for him?**
> He (S.D. Burman) would always say to my father, 'Bikram, this girl has such a beautiful voice, you are spoiling her voice. You should let her sing in films.'
>
> 'But Dada,' my father would protest, 'she's still in

school, she has her exams, how can I let her sing for films?'

'Oh come on, one film will not do her any harm,' he would retort. It was probably the outcome of one such conversation that led to my singing for him finally.

Meena also goes on to say that she was in awe of Sachin Kaka, as he was so senior to her in age and stature. But he on his part never stinted in helping her learn the song to bring out its melody in the best possible way. He would play the song on the harmonium and sing it and she would follow. 'The other quality I found notable about him is his emphasis on phonetics,' she adds. 'I remember for my first film him directing Raja Mehdi Ali Khan to write phonetically pleasing words with his own examples. That is why I always feel his songs sound so pleasing.'

Simple words and lilting tunes, new voices trained and tuned to show off their uniqueness to advantage, Sachin Dev Burman would make these the hallmark signatures in his long career in Hindi films.

34

I realize I am finding new paths in this city where I live and work. If I cannot walk about at will in these crowds, and fear being knocked down by the fast-moving cars and horse carts, at least my mind is doing what my body cannot.

My music, I realize, will not bow to any compromise. I seek new frontiers, new voices, new expressions. Others may be happy with established singers; and I use their voices too, they are remarkable. But I seek new talent to find voices I can mould and shape and use to express exactly what I want in my song. New voices are malleable, each singer can be shown how to use his or her voice differently from others, in a way that is unique.

The other day, someone asked me if I did not care for singers and that I choose them as one would vegetables in the market, trying one or the other. I replied, 'Of course I care for them, but I care for my song more. I must use the voice that suits the song and the scene best. Only then is the entire thing perfect.'

My search for new voices is relentless. My ear is always tuned to a fresh sound, free of imitation.

Sometimes it works, pays rich dividends; other times, nothing.

In that girl, Geeta Roy, I have found a real treasure. What a voice she has, capable of communicating emotion at its every pitch. Even I did not imagine that the songs I gave her in *Do Bhai* would be such hits.

A chit of a girl, what does she know of life, but she sang the songs with such feeling, the words were steeped in pathos. You could hear her world crashing, the recordist told me, when she sang '*Mera sundar sapna beet gaya*' with a catch in her voice. It came to her naturally, almost like a flaw, but it perfected the song. Even the producer had to step back and acknowledge he had erred in underestimating her vocal flexibility. True, when he first heard her she had rough edges, which I smoothed out, but here was a diamond if there was any. I want her to sing all my songs. She is ripe for new experiments with her voice.

The Kapoor boy, Raj, however might never make it as a singer. He sang the song I taught him quite well, but I think his passion lies elsewhere. I hear he is directing his first film. I don't think he will sing for me or anyone else again, not unless his film fails and he has to restrain himself as a director and stick to acting and perhaps, singing.

As I said, some gambles result in great gain, others in loss.

♬

Incidentally, a little-known fact is that among SD's assistants for *Do Bhai* was a musical-minded ex-army man, who would later blaze his own trail as a composer of evergreen melodies. His name: Madan Mohan.

35

One gamble that would work for him would be Manna Dey.

It was as if destiny was watching, playing a strange game with the man it had gifted with the joy of music.

He had crossed the frontiers from Bengali music to a music that would have no regional borders. His background was rich and varied and layered enough to let him make a tune that could lift the spirits, or cause a heaviness in the listener's heart. His successes were big enough to put him on par with many of his more savvy contemporaries, men like Naushad and Shankar-Jaikishan who strode unafraid into a world where melody and rhythm waited for their batons to bring them to life on singers' lips.

The wheel of fortune, however, turned strangely for S.D.

Burman. One minute he was shining like the star he was; then there was nothing. Was he a flash in the sky? A comet whose brilliance would vanish with one streak across the filmic firmament?

The films had come thick and fast after the success of *Do Bhai*. There had been *Vidya*, and *Kamal* and *Shabnam*. But only the last film, *Shabnam*, made some impact with the listeners. He had also made his first music compositions for the newly created company called Navketan, which was floated by the Anand brothers, Chetan, Goldie and Dev. Though a well-made film, with songs that made waves, *Afsar* was a financial disaster. As the banner's first film, it did not portend well for Navketan, and gave no intimation of the fact that it would fly long and triumphantly well into the future.

Even *Pyar*, which followed with Kishore Kumar singing his first solo for S.D. Burman, did not break any new ground. S.D. Burman's experiments with new voices were still hit-and-miss affairs, and it seemed to be the turn of the misses.

The music of other films, by other directors, was far, far more successful. He felt he had lost his moorings and his abilities. The place was alien to him still, he had not got under Bombay's skin, not understood its needs.

Calcutta beckoned. He had created endless hits there; had a fan following that was unquestionable. They missed him, he missed his city.

He would pack up his ambitions of being a composer for Hindi films and leave. He bought his ticket, and prepared for the journey.

♫

In life some people have a definite role as catalysts. They come in for a purpose, stepping in and out of one's life as if on cue, at crucial moments.

The biographies of great men always show this play of some pivotal character in the twists and turns their creative life takes. So it is in our lives too, though we may not be aware of it. Someone we respect, or sometimes don't even really think as important, comes in at an opportune moment and changes the course of our thoughts, or the flow of our destiny, forever.

Thus it was that actor Ashok Kumar came again into S.D. Burman's life.

Ashok Kumar was shooting for *Mashaal* at the time when S.D. Burman, the man he had helped find a foothold in Bombay, was packing his bags to go back to Calcutta. Hoping to entice him to stay longer–because Ashok Kumar knew he was talented and should not be allowed to give up so easily–the actor asked the composer to create the music for *Mashaal*.

Work had started, but SD was still unhappy. He decided to hand over the baton to his assistant Manna Dey, who was an admirer and student and of course the nephew of his erstwhile guru K.C. Dey, and leave.

But Ashok Kumar was persuasive. And SD stayed. And changed the course of his destiny. As well as that of Manna Dey.

36

Manna Dey has gone on record often enough to retell the story of his first song for S.D. Burman. It is a tale worth repeating, though. Here is an excerpt from his own story printed in the S.D. Burman Birth Centenary Commemorative Souvenir, as narrated in an interview with Satish Kalra in New Jersey: 'After finishing my graduation, I migrated to Bombay in 1943. The Bombay film world was totally different, the way of doing music there was tough and specialized, and I devoted a lot of time to learning. In this period I was an assistant to many stalwarts like Anil Biswas, Khemchand Prakash, my uncle, and Burman Saab. I worked as Burman-da's assistant in Bombay Talkies Films. In *Mashaal* I was credited as assistant music director. Those were great days.'

He did not say it in so many words in this particular interview, but the history of music in Indian cinema has it that Manna often wondered why he was never given a break as a singer by his Dada, whose style of singing he so admired and who was his own uncle's student.

Was his fate as Dada's assistant to only rehearse others and never sing? He had indeed sung for other music composers, but he wondered why his own master was ignoring him. Would he never ever give him a break?

The break, when it came, broke all records. Still prepared to go back to Calcutta, S.D. Burman, however, gave the job on hand his complete attention. As was his wont, he prepared many tunes for each situation, and let the producer choose the one he thought would fit best.

As for the voices, he would choose whichever voice he thought would work best for the song.

And that is how Manna came to sing.

The song, '*Upar gagan vishal*', was of a different genre. It was not a romantic ditty, it was a song that was a commentary, an exhortation. It needed an open, clear-throated voice that would not be identified easily–what could be called a voice in the K.C. Dey style of singing. S.D. Burman knew well that the guru's nephew was trained in the same tradition as himself, and could sing the song exactly as was required of him.

So it was that one morning, Manna Dey heard himself being called by his master, not to buy chanachoor, or to help prepare another singer, but to rehearse and record a song. His surprise must have turned to delight, and then a slight nervousness at the task finally at hand. But the singer was well equipped to rise to the challenge. His master's faith in him was clearly justified. S.D. Burman knew his singers well, knew what each voice could deliver best. And Manna Dey never looked back.

'I rendered my first lines for "*Upar gagan vishal*",' Manna said in an interview with Ranjan Dasgupta in the *Hindu*. 'S.D. Burman asked me to raise my vocal octaves, maintain a lyrical balance and slowly lower my voice without any special effort. I was very convinced by his understanding of melody and followed his direction. He looked at me, then to his musicians and wielded the baton majestically. After the recording, which was over in four takes, he congratulated me, patting me on my back.'

In fact, with his very first song, in *Mashaal*, which S.D. Burman had decided would be his last endeavour in Hindi films, Manna Dey sealed his master's destiny. By delivering a hit so immense that the composer could not be allowed to turn his back on an industry that now hailed him as one of its own!

In fact, through his long career, S.D. Burman would depend

on Manna Dey for some of the most poetic and intricate compositions he created.

♫

Excerpt from S.D. Burman's autobiography Sargamer Nikhad

It is not that I have not composed any difficult and complex tunes based on classical music if the need arose. And for these my favourite artist is Sri Manna Dey, who is like a brother to me. He is the nephew of my first guru in Calcutta, late Sri Krishna Chandra Dey. Manna has been in Bombay for a long time. I was the music director for two films produced by Bombay Talkies–both the films were made based on the novel *Rajani* by Sri Bankim (Chandra) Chattopadhyay. The Bengali version was *Samar* and in Hindi the name was *Mashaal*. For both the films, Nitin-da was the director and Ashok Kumar was the hero. Manna was my assistant music director. He is a very modest, unselfish and soft-spoken person. Bombay film music now has become a bit mechanical, the artists are busy recording every day, and there is hardly any time left for practice. But Manna is an exception. Even at the peak of popularity and fame he practises each morning with his tanpura; he hardly misses this routine. I am really charmed by his attachment and respect for music. Due to this, I have special affection for him. Manna has sung and is singing for me in many of my films. He can bring any song to life.

37

Walk down the road that links the arterial S.V. Road, which people once knew as Swami Vivekananda Road, to the suburban railway station at Khar station in the western suburbs of Mumbai, and you are in as bustling and congested a road as any other that runs along a station in the metropolis. Buildings vie for space with shacks and roadside vendors sell everything from plastic chappals to vegetables and fruit. The air can tempt you with the fragrance of bhajiyas frying in hot oil at one step, and repel you with the odour of unclaimed rubbish, the next. Sounds assail your ears. The honking of horns, the thud-thud of two wheelers, the yelping of a street dog hit by a vagrant's stone, and sometimes a snatch of music from a roadside eatery are a regular part of the background noise.

If perchance you pass by when the song being played is one of S.D. Burman's compositions, it would be a strange coincidence, serendipity indeed. For it was on this street that the composer had once set up his base.

Walk a bit further down and you might pass Hotel Evergreen. Nothing sets it apart from the others that usually line roads near stations. But look closely and the number 1946 will strike your gaze. The hotel was obviously built in that year! This is the place where S.D. Burman and wife Meera shared a room with a balcony, Room 19 to be exact, paying 160 rupees as rental, though today many years since, the room must surely look very different, to merit the Rs 2500 rental it now commands.

Maybe it was its modest layout that attracted S.D. Burman, as it did many others who were just stepping into a career in films. The rooms were clean, and for eighty rupees per head, boarders could also enjoy tea, breakfast, lunch and evening meals. And even more inviting was the offer of bed tea!

Today, no sound of music or words pertaining to scenes from films in the making might float out of Room 19 to greet the ears of the residents traversing the corridors of Hotel Evergreen, but in that time, the sound of the dholak, as SD sat playing it, was common, as were the sound of voices discussing the results of a football match or a game of tennis.

38

Suddenly he was surrounded by like-minded people. People connected with making films, with different aspects of cinema, but all seeking the same thing he sought. Integrity and excellence.

Among the young and passion-filled minds he now came into contact with was a young poet. Abdul Hayee, new to the city, trying to find his space in the writing world that yet ignored him despite his success at a Progressive Writers' Conference in 1949, where he had met luminiaries like Ismat Chughtai and Jan Nisar Akhtar. Prem Dhawan, who had befriended him, tried to help him by sending his poems to significant members of the film fraternity.

Writing under the pen name, Sahir Ludhianvi, the poet was exactly what SD was looking for. He was impassioned, he was idealistic, and he was looking for a break. Quick to spot potential, the composer signed him on for the two films he was working on, *Naujawan* and *Baazi*.

Sahir's composition *'Thandi hawaein'* for *Naujawan* captured the freshness of young love; it was a gentle breeze that floated on S.D. Burman's music and, wrapped in Lata's fresh voice, it swayed the heart of a generation looking for new dreams of love. Both lyricist and composer tasted the sweetness of success with the song.

Yet, with his next film, S.D. Burman was faced with a puzzle.

The scene was the first that would be shot for *Baazi*. Guru Dutt would direct the film, his very first as a director. The result of an understanding between two out-of-work hopefuls, *Baazi* starred Dev Anand while his friend Dutt wielded the megaphone.

The scene was a complex one to start a film with for a new director, but Guru Dutt obviously wanted to use his skills as a choreographer, learnt at no less an institution than Uday Shankar's at Almora, to good use.

It was a delicately balanced scene. A song, shot on the gangster's moll, who was to seduce the hero. Yet she was obviously half in love with the debonair, dashingly handsome young man, and even as she sang to him to lure him along, she wished to warn him of the dangers lurking around.

Sahir jumped into the scene with fervour, he had written a ghazal for this scene. It was S.D. Burman's turn now!

♫

Burman is given the entire history of the ghazal in brief. A ghazal has a certain metre, a definite structure. And most important, a mood. It is strict in the way it follows all this. A ghazal is a series of couplets, and the couplets always rhyme.

And there is a constant refrain that recurs in the second couplet. The mood is romantic, sometimes full of pain.

And the song therefore must be also slow and beautiful. Perhaps indicative of pain.

He has taken the lesson and the scene home as it has been described to him. He carries it in his mind, like a precious vessel full of nectar, he dare not let it go, in case he spills the contents, the explanations.

He has tried to find out the storyline and why the girl is singing and to whom.

It is the very first scene to be shot for the film, the muhurat shot. It makes him proud that his song will be part of the muhurat, and filmed on Geeta Bali, who is quite a big star.

He mulls over what he has learnt, though he is not sure of the complete veracity of what he has been told.

A girl singing to herself, and half to the man she wishes to communicate a message of love to, a man she is in love with. His life could be in danger, he might be killed. And in her heart is sorrow, and love.

He mulls over the song, the tune. Tries various tunes, some make him want to weep, would that be nice, he wonders, making the audience weep for the maiden so hopelessly in love? Or should there be some dread, some vague foreboding, to signify danger, a clash of cymbals perhaps, or the strumming of a sitar?

Na, the sitar would not work, this is a Western setting. Gangsters, he reminds himself, they don't have sitars and flutes. Think different. Think Western.

He puts the song away.

Over dinner he discusses the song with Meera. Perhaps she

would have a suggestion. You can do it, is all Meera says, her mind preoccupied perhaps with matters of the kitchen.

I must involve her more in my work, he thinks, and remembers they have songs to sing when they go back to Calcutta. But in this, his Hindi compositions, she has little to say. I must draw her into this part of my work, he tells himself again.

The scene will not leave him. He needs an instrument. Yes, that will make things easy. If it was Western, a guitar would have to be the right instrument. Or a violin.

A violin would have the right pathos.

He thinks it over, but the visual does not work right for him. He decides to discuss it with Dutt the next day. Will a violin work better or a guitar?

The song would then follow the instrument.

39

Six years later, after creating songs for *Pyaasa*, songs that still move hearts with the force of their poetry and the beauty of their melodies, the partnership between S.D. Burman and Sahir Ludhianvi would shatter–over a clash of egos.

As coins that jingle together in the same pocket may find their contours erased by friction, so it was with the two men who had strong ideas about themselves, their legacies and their place in the world of music.

S.D. Burman, never one to compromise on his work, given entirely to his music and his own way of life, stood at one end. Sahir, poet, rebel, proud of his 'metre' and yet harbouring deep insecurities as poets sometimes do, was sure of his ground and how he stood tall on it.

The feud in *Pyaasa* broke over which was the more creative field. Poetry or song. Of course S.D. Burman felt it was the song that ruled, that set the pace for the poem, the words only helped articulate the music. Without words, the music would still please, it would move souls as only music could do, even in a film scene. Poetry, on the other hand, often needed the embellishment of music to reach the ear of the common man. Without music, poetry would languish unheard, as something only a connoisseur could enjoy. Using this as an argument perhaps, S.D. Burman had managed to create the precedent of setting a tune first and then handing it over for the lyricist to fill in with words.

But in *Pyaasa*, Sahir turned the tables on Dada. He had words ready, a song named chakla, and the metre was set. There would be no change. Dada was forced to set the words to tune, there was no way out.

This must have rankled, as also the fact that he sincerely believed that the tune was more powerful than the word. The last straw was Sahir's insistence on being paid a rupee more than S.D. Burman. Sahir was a proud man, his name was already ringing in the halls of fame, as one of India's best. He had as many hits to his credit as any other writer, and his contribution to S.D. Burman's success was immense. SD refused to bend to the caveat and walked out of the relationship.

♫

But that is much later. Whatever the discussion between Guru Dutt, the director of *Baazi*, and its music director touched upon, the fact remains that on the day of the recording, the song that was presented had the girl strumming a guitar and singing, not a soulful ditty, but a Western jazzy tune.

Sahir was young, and new. It was his second recording with S.D. Burman. Their first act together for *Naujawan* had offered a tremendous hit in the Lata song '*Thandi hawaein*'. There was reason to believe they would work well this time too. But when faced with the strange interpretation of his ghazal, Sahir's angst was unbearable. He did not care that he was still making his mark, that S.D. Burman was a name of some repute. Upset and beside himself, he decided to walk out of the film. His temper would always be his companion, it had always been his undoing. This time too it almost was.

As K.K. Paul reports in the *Hindustan Times* of 8 March 2012, Sahir's ninetieth birth anniversary, if Geeta Dutt had not taken him aside and spoken to him, and smoothed his ego and his temper, filmic history might have taken quite a different turn.

Of course, history records that the song, '*Tadbeer se bigdi hui taqdeer bana le*', went on to become one of the film's biggest draws. Geeta Bali, in the role of vamp, a gangster's moll, rolled her eyes with such dexterous, hidden messages in them, and sang the song with such joie de vivre, that audiences would sit through the film till the song came up, and leave soon after!

Though he set the tune as he thought best, pushing the frontier so to say even as he pushed his own knowledge to new limits, S.D. Burman was nervous about the outcome of his composition when it would finally be shown on screen. The story goes that he was so worried that he took off on a holiday out of Bombay to sit quietly fishing through the days and spend his evenings watching the sunset, hoping to avoid any brickbats aimed his way.

It was only when he heard some kids splashing in the waters and actually mouthing the words and humming the tune of '*Tadbeer se...*' that he folded his fishing pole and wended his way back into the city.

♫

Baazi proved to be a milestone for S.D. Burman. It proved he could turn something upside down and yet make it work wonderfully. In the process of making a ghazal a Western number, he also helped expand the range of Geeta Dutt's voice. This 'rediscovery' of Geeta Dutt would free her from the narrow confines of the sad songs and bhajans that she was being slotted into.

One more offshoot of *Baazi* was that the director Guru Dutt fell in love with his singer, and they were married two years later, to continue a great creative collaboration that worked despite the turbulence of their married life.

40

Rasogullas in our mouth – that is what they say I speak with when I speak Hindi in this city. What do they know of the sweetness of Bangla, with its vowel endings and rounded vowel sounds. Even a gaali sounds musical in it. And I am not the only one who speaks making aas into oos. I think most Bangla speakers do that. My new singer Hemanta

Mukhopadhyay also does it. But what a voice. It is like silk, a different silk from Talat, which is soft and sheer like Meera's sari which they gave her for her birthday, something called chiffon. Hemant's voice is like Bhagalpur silk, heavy. You can hear it rustling, you can feel its weight, and the words get a new depth when he sings them. The sonorous quality of his voice is so well suited to soft romantic songs, the lullabies, and I think he can even sing patriotic numbers. The background of Rabindra Sangeet makes it easy for him to be so melodious, his voice is like a boat gliding on the water on a moonlit night. When he lifts the sur, it goes gliding smoothly into the next octave. Only his pronunciation needs to be corrected. And some of the rawness has to be smoothened out.

I am gaining a reputation as someone who upsets the balance, I think. Even Guru Dutt has started to think this, and though I respect and love him, I cannot but stick to what I believe is right for my song.

Guru wants Talat to sing the song. Of course it will sound good, Talat is inimitable. But I feel this song is right for Hemant. He will bring the right mood, his voice will make the words come alive, listeners will see the moon over the waves when he sings the words '*leheron ki chaaon mein, khoyi khoyi chandni...*'

Hemant has not sung solo before. I used him in *Saaza* in one duet with Sandhya Mukhopadhyay. I think their voices worked well, but his enunciation was still very accented. Sandhya has gone back, but Hemant is still here. He respects me as a music director and admitted as much, adding that he was a fan of my singing even when in Calcutta. I never knew it till now, but he was part of the group of boys who gathered outside to listen to my riyaz in the mornings!

He would be a sincere pupil and learn whatever I wished to teach him about singing in Hindi films, he said. I like his humility; it shows that his talent is a tool that he will use only for the good of music, that he will bend and blend as the song requires. I think he has great potential, and can be trained. I have been working with him, he has worked very hard, I told Guru, 'He will sing this song.'

To say Guru was shocked is a joke. I thought he would faint. His face was flushed and his ears turned red. But he admires and respects me too much to say anything directly. He only laughed, and left the room.

♫

History reports that Hemanta's dedication and rehearsing paid off. As did S.D. Burman's faith in the new singer. Though *Jaal* had many lovely hummable numbers, the solo by the silky-voiced lover wooed more hearts than just the heroine's, scoring in popularity even over the duet of the same song. The only reason he was not fixed as the actor's only voice was SD's insistence on having a singer who would do justice to the tune rather than simply opting for a voice that would match the hero's or heroine's.

It was a trait that would later get for Hemant the other hit number, still hummed today, from *Pyaasa*, '*Jaane woh kaise log the jinke pyar ko pyar mila*'.

Though the rest of the songs filmed on Guru Dutt in *Pyaasa* were sung by Rafi, and though Guru Dutt's assistant director in the film, and its writer, Abrar Alvi has gone on record saying Hemanta was his suggestion for the song, the fact remains that Dada Burman endorsed the view. Or it would never have been Hemant's voice that sung the song.

To digress a bit: if Hemanta literally snatched a song from Talat in *Jaal*, he would be subjected to the same fate in a later film.

R.D. Burman says in an interview to *Screen* in 1995 that though he was personally in favour of Hemant singing '*Chal ri sajni*' in *Bombai Ka Babu*, his father insisted Mukesh should voice the song. And Mukesh it was.

The fact remains that both Hemant Kumar and Mukesh were great for background songs, as was S.D. Burman himself.

Hemant Kumar's first recorded solo for a film called *Irada* had gone unnoticed, and S.D. Burman is today credited with giving the music director, who had come to work for Filmistan studio, his first break as playback singer. The singer would reward the trust reposed in him by rendering with utmost dedication and pure virtuosity hit numbers for the Burman baton, for *House Number 44*. Among them '*Chup hai dharti, chup hai chand sitare*', and the plaintive '*Teri duniya mein jeene se*' quite making up for saying nothing more than oho and aha to Lata's '*Peechhe peechhe aakan*' in the same film.

41

The moonlight rides the waves as they hit against the shore. The hero sits at the edge of the water, his full-sleeved shirt is open at the neck, his pants are immaculately pleated. Poor he may be, just a taxi driver, but he has style. The song he sings is sad, despondent as the night, unlit by the moon – in sharp contrast, the waves shine like silver taunting him with their brightness.

When he looks up, turning his face to the heavens in despair, the moonlight caresses his face, outlining his features; his eyes speak of sorrow, his song of despair. Talat Mahmood's voice adds the right mood, the words flow in perfect harmony, the catch in the throat of the singer finds itself repeated in the catch in his voice that swells in the throats of those watching the scene.

It is essential S.D. Burman: the water, the moon, the strains of the flute that weave the song together. It culls from his boyhood memories, the scene could be his own life, and the tune comes alive.

In another segment, the heroine, Kalpana Kartik, sings the same song. Lata sings it with more classical overtones, there is even an alaap thrown in, but the scene is more prosaic, centring more on the actors rather than giving the song a chance to stand on its own.

Chetan Anand directs the female version with a sense of drama, Dev Anand's song is pure visual poetry that creates a moving scene.

Little wonder the song won for S.D. Burman his first Filmfare Award.

Yet the story goes that S.D. Burman did not compose the tune while sitting by the sea. It came to him, as his tunes were wont to doing, when he was doing something else. While driving home from a friend's house, he lost his way, and found the tune instead. The song, '*Jaayen toh jaayen kahan*', is based on the Rabindra Sangeet, '*Hey khoniker otithi*'.

Taxi Driver, like *Baazi*, was to make cinematic history. The lead pair would marry, the film would set a landmark as being among the first to show Bombay as a real city with the poor hero being just a taxi driver with a high sense of romance, and S.D. Burman would reach a point where he would vanquish all competition at the awards, beating his friend and nearest competitor Naushad to the finish line without any trouble.

Of such simple moments is cinematic history made!

But it would take another twenty years before he won his next Filmfare Award–such is the history of film awards!

42

Cinematic history is replete with films that compete against themselves. A theme recurs, having caught the imagination of viewers and writers alike; film-makers find they are pulled to it as if to a magnet. Love stories of historical characters are among these. The fateful tragedy of the doomed love of Anarkali and Prince Salim is one oft-repeated tale that has had generations of moviegoers reaching for their handkerchiefs. And even as directors vie to make their creation stand out over the competition, music composers and lyricists try to ensure that theirs is the song that will linger in memory long after the scenes are forgotten.

Stories of Naushad and Shakeel Badayuni trying to create a song for Anarkali to sing in K Asif's *Mughal-e-Azam* that would be more powerful than the record-breaking '*Muhabbat mein aise kadam dagmagaye*' in the hit 1953 film *Anarkali*, tell of how they chanced upon the now-iconic challenge lovers throw at society even today, where Anarkali challenges Akbar with '*Pyar kiya to darna kya*'. Sitting up all night, struggling to create the song, it was Shakeel who finally sighed and said something about being unafraid once they had thrown the gauntlet and entered the ring. The tune followed and the words wove themselves, as the mood spelt it all out.

The fictional story of Devdas has another such theme. Writer Sarat Chandra might never have dreamt that his besotted, liquor-soaked loser of a protagonist would become such a cult figure thanks to film-makers immortalizing his angst on screen.

Devdas was the story that presented itself to S.D. Burman now. Bimal Roy, Bengali to the core, working with writer Nabendu Ghosh, decided that only another Bengali soul could capture the essence of the love story, steeped as it was in the flavour of early twentieth-century Bengal.

Inherent in the enterprise was the challenge it held. Bimal Roy would walk a path taken by a director before him, who was practically an icon himself besides being his guru, and had created history with his production. And S.D. Burman would have to pit his might against the joint melody of three stalwarts who had created musical history with the songs that Saigal had sung: R.C. Boral, Pankaj Mullick and Timir Baran.

SD remembered with a pang how, in 1935, Mullick had ousted him, using Pahari Sanyal's voice over his own for the final recording for a song in the film *Yahudi ki Ladki*. By getting the golden-voiced Saigal to play Devdas and sing the laments of unrequited, lost love, director Pramathesh Barua had claimed the imagination of an entire nation. Would Bimal Roy ever match that greatness? Would S.D. Burman? Could anyone hope to outdo Saigal?

Doubtless, these thoughts must have hung like a miasma over the four men–Bimal Roy, SD, Ghosh and Sahir–while they worked to shape the many aspects of the film which had Dilip Kumar playing the title role and Calcutta's Suchitra Sen playing Paro. Vyjayanthimala, the dancing beauty from the south, would play Chandramukhi. It was a gamble, but the die was cast. The show had to go on!

43

Meera is right. I must stop and think. She is gentle and full of love but I think I sensed a reproach in her voice yesterday. We were preparing to sleep. I was undoing my little treasure packet of paan, to end the day with the sweetness of the juices of leaf and nut in my mouth. The meal was sumptuous; I wondered if I had forgotten some occasion that merited the extra dishes that I was served. I tend to be forgetful of the small but important things in life these days.

I think I understand now, Meera was telling me through the food that she cared, but had to say what she said later.

'I was going too fast, she said, did I not think so?'

I replied, no, it has been a long wait, and now that the struggle was paying off, it was only right that I make the most and reap in the rewards.

'Twenty-three films in less than four years,' she said softly. 'Is that not a lot?' It stopped me short. Were there really that many, I had never stopped to count, just gone on from one assignment to another, one song to another, surrounding my life, my mind, my home in music.

Having Tublu around is like a spur. He sits watching me, listening to me. The boy is talented; he just needs to discipline himself. And when he listens I want to set an example, give my best.

Twenty-three, I mused. That is a lot. After *Baazi*, the offers had started coming in, so many films, so many songs. Some did well, made me happy. But now when I look back, I realize there were many that never became a hit as big as *Baazi*. Maybe *Jaal*, and now *Taxi Driver*. Maybe she is right. I must exercise discretion.

'I am happy you will do *Devdas*.' Meera's voice was still soft, low. Her eyes shone in the half-light, I could sense her happiness as she spoke of it, but was there something else. She went on, 'It is a big challenge. You and I both know how accomplished a writer Nabendu Babu is, and Bimal Roy is expecting a lot from the film. Your songs will have to be really powerful. You must give the film the respect and time it needs.'

I was about to say that I always do, but I bit my tongue. Deep in my heart I knew *Devdas* would be a bridge that would either take me right across or drop me into the rushing waters of failure.

An artiste in Hindi films is as good as his last work. This is a truth that cannot be denied.

'You are probably right,' I said to Meera as I lay down against the pillows. Suddenly I was tired. The task was enormous. She placed her cool hand on my forehead. 'It's a beautiful story, layered with emotion and poetry. Your songs will accentuate the magic and make it even more powerful,' she said. 'All you need to do is think fresh, think different. Go back to the classical. The story demands it.' I looked at Meera in surprise, my pupil wife was really being my master now!

'I think you speak wisely,' I said.

That night the tabla never stopped playing in my head.

44

Dedicated to his guru, Barua, by Bimal Roy, the 1955 version of *Devdas* was a tapestry of intense emotion, riveting music and a storyline that ran true to the text, yet added nuances and pathos that only a visual medium could bring. Playing up the contrast between the two actresses who played the two women in Devdas's life, the film moved through shades of sorrow to deeper despair to finally end in the heart-rending scene of the hero's death. The suffering of the two women who loved Devdas in their own different ways, would continue, and linger in the theatre even after the lights came on.

The film gave enough musical scope for any composer to create to his heart's content. Bhajans and dances, songs of the road and of parting–S.D. Burman had perhaps never been given such a blank canvas to fill.

If Bimal Roy could visualize songs that would become trendsetters for eons to come in the way they were shot, Dada Burman was no less involved in ensuring the music he created perfectly suited the scene. For him, always, the story was paramount. He had to know everything about the scene he was writing the music for, and what the mood of it was, the characters in it, the movement. In fact, there is every chance that he had his little nuggets of ideas to give too, while the scene was being shot, or visualized. Both Bimal Roy and S.D. Burman shared the Bengal background, and the common sight of Vaishnav bhajan singers singing their way through a town as they walked their path seeking salvation and God must have been part of their subconscious. Both Bimal Roy and S.D. Burman believed a song was not only a song, and was more than just a pause, in a story. A song was a means to carrying the story forward, of expressing emotions that words and dialogues could not. The nuances of a song could reach the heart faster than a scene with mere dialogue in it.

♫

Geeta Dutt: *Aan milo, aan milo, Shyaam Saanvare / Brij mein akeli raadhe khoi-khoi phire.*
Manna Dey: *O Raadhe khoi-khoi phire, O Kaanha, aan milo.*

If Manna Dey was S.D. Burman's choice for songs that created background atmosphere, Geeta Dutt was not far behind. Her voice had the capacity to rise to a point where it reached the universal, rather than being part of the individual.

As the song unfolds, the story takes a leap, as the young Paro identifies herself with Radha and discovers the yearning in her heart. If the lyrics were indicative of yearning, the pull of the music on the heart combined with the visual made the scene memorable both to the film lover and to a generation of film-makers who were each trying to break new ground.

Two years later, Guru Dutt would use a similar device in *Pyaasa* with '*Aaj sajan mohe aang laga lo*', taking the scene forward to show us the blossoming of adoration in Gulabo's heart for the poet who had saved her from the law, and whose poems she already adored. S.D. Burman would again use the same source to create another bhajan that would reverberate in the heart of the listener long after the scene.

It is not possible so many years later for anyone to conjecture if one scene influenced the other. After all, Guru Dutt too was a Bengali at heart, and had enough of the Bengal background to know of travelling minstrels. And to him too a song was more than just a song, it was visual poetry to take the story to the next step.

Devdas veered between the city and the village, and S.D. Burman, perhaps, more than most of his contemporaries, was well equipped to deal with the needs of both environs. For Chandramukhi's thumris, SD delved into the layers of classical learning that he had imbibed. Using ragas that suited the scene and the emotion of the lyrics by Sahir, the tunes would dance their way into the listener's consciousness.

SD used Lata's voice for the thumri numbers on Vyjayanthimala; their intricacies of mood and rhythm was best articulated by the singer whose voice simply glided over the complex patterns of the ragas, making them seem simple and hummable. SD had learnt his lesson well over the years: even thumris needed to be hummable and not seem formidable pieces of serious music, even as they maintained the purity of the chosen raga.

Rafi, already a big name in male voices, and the lesser-known Mubarak Begum were also given songs. SD stuck to his theory that a singer who could best interpret a tune would be the right voice for a song, and used five voices for the ten songs of *Devdas*.

One of the most exceptional compositions in *Devdas* is the plaintive '*Mitwa*', which S.D. Burman assigned to Talat Mahmood to sing. Sahir's poem is set in a classical raga and the ghazal maestro's tremulous voice blends perfectly with the weeping sarangi in the background. Only the flute and the sitar offer relief, and the distant rumble of thunder is the perfect foil to the visual of mango groves and the river flowing past. Breaking away from the usual mukhda-antara structure of the film song, the music is a sigh of suppressed agony breaking free to find expression.

♫

Excerpt from S.D. Burman's autobiography Sargamer Nikhad

Bimal-da had a very pleasant and attractive personality. We knew each other from the era of New Theatres at Calcutta and enjoyed cordial relations. I directed music for four of his movies (*Devdas*, *Sujata*, *Bandini* and *Benazir*) and enjoyed it enormously. Bimal-da was a 'blind admirer' of my music.

Generally, he was never absent during any of my musical programmes. In spite of being a great director, he always respected my decisions regarding the music and its situations in the films. He would never force his views upon me. If I disagreed with his views regarding the music in any film, he would accept my ideas. As an example, I can recall a situation for a song in the film *Sujata*.

I suggested that after the scene at Gandhi Ghat, Sujata should go back home. After some time, Adhir makes a call to Sujata and sings a love song over the telephone. This created a very dramatic situation. The audience effusively applauded the song and praised me for it.

45

A year later, S.D. Burman finds himself less busy. One single film in hand – *Funtoosh*.

It would do for the exuberant, ebullient Kishore Kumar what '*Tadbeer se bigdi hui*' had done for Geeta Dutt. Only in reverse. '*Tadbeer se bigdi hui*' had helped Geeta Dutt break the image of a singer of soulful songs and bhajans. '*Dukhi man mere*' broke the mould Kishore had been cast thus far in, of a fun-loving, untrained voice that could breeze through songs with uncanny zest.

The sombre, slow notes of '*Dukhi man mere*' brought out the rich timbre of the youthful singer's voice, and despite his lack of classical training, allowed him to express both expertise and emotion. The song would bring tears to many an eye watching the screen, thanks not only to the hero's disarming looks that broke hearts when he was downcast, but also thanks to the rich subtext of emotion layered by the singer of the song.

The success of the song established Kishore Kumar as a singer of no mean standing and extreme versatility, and it gave S.D. Burman reason to believe that Dev Anand would best sing in the voice of Kishore Kumar. At least for Navketan Films. The Talat and Rafi phase for Dev would soon give way to the new voice of Kishore Kumar. But, Dada would still stand by his belief in the suitability of a song to a singer and in classic numbers in *Kala Paani*, *Kala Bazaar*, *Tere Ghar Ke Saamne* and *Guide* would fall back on Rafi as Dev Anand's singing voice.

46

New stars were shining in every segment of Hindi films. Directors like Chetan Anand and Vijay Anand were coming to the forefront; Guru Dutt was establishing himself as a creator of films that would not be easily forgotten. Moving away from his old swashbuckling, devil-may-care image, he was taking a risky and big gamble with his new film *Pyaasa*, based on a streetwalker's story. Playing the role of the streetwalker, opposite the director himself, was a young starlet from the south, Waheeda Rehman.

S.D. Burman had a clutch of films on hand all of a sudden. It was as if *Funtoosh* had opened a valve in the dam of success. *Paying Guest*, *Miss India*, *Nau Do Gyarah* – three other films, each different from the other, vied with his work in *Pyaasa*. Only a magician could juggle all these many-coloured films in the air and keep them from flopping to the ground. The music of each demanded a different treatment. Claiming his place in the pantheon of lyric writers was another new poet, Majrooh Sultanpuri. SD would work with him in two of these three films.

Paying Guest was a film tinged with suspense and projected the contrasting personas of Dev Anand and Nutan. *Nau Do Gyarah*, styled by Vijay Anand, was a fast-paced, light film full of twists and turns, and included a heroine who spent a sizable portion of the film dressed as a man. For both, S.D. Burman created songs brimming with melody and meaning, yet as different one from the other as if two different composers had worked on the two films. And many of these songs have stood the test of time with radio channels in the new millennium airing them time and again.

But it was *Pyaasa* with which he outdid himself, working on it as if in a zone–something he would be able to do again and again with films like *Guide* and *Abhimaan*, later.

Quite unaware of the emotional drama that would wreck the lives of the two women who were the key players of his song, S.D. Burman brought in Geeta Dutt as the voice of Waheeda as he composed the song which introduces the actress for the first time to the audience and the hero. It is a teasing seductive song, and the director had the actress fully clothed, seducing both the hero and the audience with her eyes. The song was lilting in its melody and would go down in the annals of Guru Dutt Films as one of the best seduction scenes. In fact, Shankar–Jaikishan, composers of innumerable hits, especially for Raj Kapoor's banner RK Films, would be motivated to tell themselves that they would indeed have to work twice as hard to keep up with the kind of music *Pyaasa* had put out.

Perhaps the fact that Guru Dutt and S.D. Burman worked out scenes and songs together so closely helped set the trend for how most of the directors who worked with the composer would work with him. S.D. Burman was already a well-respected name in the industry by the time *Pyaasa* was being shot. Guru Dutt shared a very special relationship with Dada Burman, full of mutual respect.

Waheeda speaks in an interview by Peeyush Sharma, courtesy Moti Lalwani, of how, during the shooting of *Pyaasa*, Dada Burman would visit the sets to discuss the shot divisions or screenings or if any change was needed in his music. He would interact with Guru Dutt mostly, sometimes with V.K. Murthy and very little with others. It was very intriguing as she saw Burman Dada suggest a music piece and Guru Dutt perform a dance movement impromptu. Waheeda said she has not seen such a thing happen in the industry ever again.

Three years down the line, Vijay Anand would do much the same…

While shooting Navketan's *Kala Bazaar* (1960), they were all sitting and finalizing a Waheeda song. On the sets at Filmistan studios, Burman Dada suggested a few dance steps and Vijay Anand summoned Waheeda to come and check out. Burman Dada suggested about eight or nine different dance steps for Waheeda to choose from. When she picked the one she liked the most, he composed the entire song '*Sach huye sapne tere*' then and there to be sung by Asha in the film. Waheeda adds that the song remains one of her favourite numbers.

Once again in *Guide*, Vijay Anand, taking on the direction of the film for the home banner, would repeat the pattern.

In each of the films, S.D. Burman used voices he thought best suited to the scene and song. Kishore Kumar teased '*Mana janab ne pukara nahin*' in *Paying Guest*, an anthem that roadside Romeos would adopt for years to come; Lata wept to the moonlit night of her loneliness in '*Chand phir nikla*' in the same film; but it was Asha Bhonsle he turned to for the rollicking, mischievous numbers in both *Paying Guest* and *Nau Do Gyarah*. And even as he patronized and promoted Kishore Kumar in the first two films, he worked hard with Rafi to lower his notes as he moulded his voice to the exquisite plaint against society in '*Yeh mehlon, yeh takhton, yeh taajon ki duniya*' in *Pyaasa* or coaxed him to render the intoxicating strains of '*Khoya khoya chand*' in *Kala Bazar*.

♫

Pyaasa would have had one song more, but for its newest star, Waheeda. It was Waheeda's second film, after *CID*; she had been signed on to play the vamp in both films, thanks to her dancing talents.

When *Pyaasa* was finally completed, director Guru Dutt decided, as was his practice, to screen it for his entire cast, and other technicians and key players of his unit, so he could get some feedback. He would ask each one turn by turn what they thought of the film.

'Everybody was there,' Waheeda said, 'Mala Sinha, Johnny Walker, everyone watched the trial seriously. He took all their opinions, listened intently. Then he came to me and my mother, who had accompanied me. He asked, "How did you like the film?"

'I replied, I liked it, but it is a very serious film. But there is a very long song, "*Rut phire, din hamaare*", that I felt brings the picture down, drags it down.

'He looked at me in silence and I elaborated: The picture is about the hero Vijay, who is a poet. But when this song comes it is as if I am crying about my woes, as the character, of course. But the picture is not about my character, it is about the hero and the song is unnecessary, it drags on. Whether it is there or not will make no difference to the story.

'Because I was a newcomer, everybody was shocked. They said, you are new, how could you say this about a song composed by Burman Dada. Then Burman Dada stood up, and I saw him clearly for the first time. Though, before the picture started Guru Dutt-ji had introduced us to everybody.

'Dada said, "Waheeda, do you know how beautiful a song it is?"

'I replied, yes, it is a beautiful song, but Guru Dutt-ji has asked us all to speak up with honesty. So my mother and I explained that we did think the song was too long and as the picture was about the hero, why should I sit around crying and singing and deflecting attention?

'Mala Sinha who was my senior took my hand and said to me, "Listen, you are asking for them to cut your song. You must never say something like this. The more we get shown on screen, the better it is for us, or for any actress. Don't voice your opinions so freely."

'But, I said, Guru Dutt-ji wanted us to be honest. To which Mala Sinha said, "So does it mean you speak up openly to someone like Burman Dada!"

'I said I am not telling Burman Dada that the song is bad, the song is very beautiful. But I just feel that it is elongating the film. My point of view is that the film is the hero's story, and the entire emphasis should be on him. Why add my song in the middle of it? That is all.

'I told Dada, I am sorry, please forgive me, I am new, I do not know what to say to whom. The song is really very good.

'Then Guru Dutt-ji said, "No, no it is okay, I asked everybody their opinion."

'He would ask everybody, even his spot boy: How was it? It was his habit, he would ask everybody, the spot boy, the camera department people, everybody. And so he had asked me too. But then, the matter ended there. The picture was released, and in the second week of its run, he cut the song. He kept the song for the first week, then cut it in the second week.

'Then he called my mother and said, "Mrs Rehman, Wah, I give it to you. In that entire trial screening you two were the only ones who told me the song needed to be cut. But, naturally, why should I pay you any heed. When the picture released I noticed that when the song came on, people were going out to smoke cigarettes, meaning they were not interested in watching the song. So you both were right absolutely. And when I went to watch the film in the theatre I felt that the song was stretching the picture, quite unnecessarily. So I said, cut it out. Even Burman-da agreed. He said, 'She is right. The song is beautiful, but in the film when it comes you feel let us step out and smoke a cigarette or have some popcorn, whatever is available. It does drag the film unnecessarily.'"

'So he cut it, and then phoned us, and we were very happy, my mother and I. Then, when I met them again, Guru Dutt-ji and Burman Dada, I said, "When I watch my movie, I watch it from the audience's point of view. I don't fall in love with myself, so that I want to be seen on screen constantly, good, bad or ugly. It should never be like that."

'He said, "You are absolutely right. But it is very good; always keep it in your mind. You are still a newcomer, you are frank, and logical. Now if someone asks you, give your frank opinion, sincere opinion. It depends on the director whether he takes your opinion or not."'

47

Aaja re pardesi, Dil tadap tadap ke keh raha hai aa bhi ja,
Suhana safar...

The entire country is swaying to the songs of *Madhumati*. Salil has outdone himself, this is his finest creation in a long and wonderful creative career.

I am happy, my heart too sways to the tunes, so simple and melodious.

People never tire of asking me why I gave away *Madhumati*. It is true I gave it away. When Bimal-da asked me to create the melody for it, I hesitated. It is wonderful working with the man, he is sensitive, and mixes intelligence with sensitivity to the right degree. 'We will create another *Devdas*,' he said, his smile like a child's at the thought. I, of course, wanted to know the story. Madhumati, I mused, what kind of a name is that, like a honey bee. 'That is madhumakkhi,' Bimal said, laughing, 'this is the name of a sweet village girl in the hills. And she falls in love with a babu, who is sent to look after the estates of a zamindar. A love story, like a fairy tale. You must bring the folk songs to it, it will go so well with the tale,' he added.

The enthusiasm in his voice was infectious. But I hesitated. Something held me back.

Let me think, I said, give me some time.

It must have hurt him a bit, my lack of enthusiasm, but that's how I am. Everyone knows it. Now Bimal-da also.

I could have told him why I wanted time, reminded him of how I had floundered for the last few minutes of the background score of *Devdas*. Suddenly as if all inspiration had left me. The climax needed a kind of music that I could not get my finger on; every tune I created seemed inadequate. Salil had stepped in, he had after all worked so closely with Bimal-da in *Do Bigha Zameen* and *Parineeta*. He knew what the director would want. I let him swing his baton, and the climax was perfect, even to my ears; it could not be better. Bimal-da gave his nod too, yes, this is good.

Now, for this story of the village girl and the shehari babu too, I thought his brand of music will be better suited. I told Bimal-da so. He was aghast for a moment. 'You can do it,' he said, 'you can make rustic tunes that will fit the story so well.' It was tempting. I could hear the flute, and the cymbals and the nagara. But I desisted, resisted, said no firmly. Let him do it, it will be perfect, I said. And Bimal-da turned on his heel and walked out slowly.

Today, I am happy that I was right. I don't think anyone could have made songs that suited the film, the actors and the scenes better than what Salil has done.

48

A few years down the line, S.D. Burman would repeat the move, handing over a film to his assistant Jaidev.

Today, reports are confused about whether Jaidev, who was invaluable to S.D. Burman as an arranger of his music, and interpreter and assistant all rolled into one, directly asked Navketan to give him the music of *Hum Dono*, or whether S.D. Burman, suffering from a bout of ill health, suggested to Navketan that his talented assistant take on the baton.

But past episodes hint that the latter may be the case. Sure of his prowess and capacity to create music that moved hearts, the maestro was secure enough to let someone else shine in his own light.

Whatever the background to Jaidev wielding the music director's baton for *Hum Dono*, he had to bow to the Anand brothers' caveat that his compositions had to be vetted by S.D.

Burman. The maestro, on his part, was of course helpful, making suggestions where he thought they would improve the music or the rendering of the song.

Jaidev's tunes for *Hum Dono* rank among his best, in fact rank among the best in the history of film music. Lata Mangeshkar, who agreed to sing for S.D. Burman's assistant because Navketan wanted her to do so and imposed the caveat on Jaidev that he get her to sing for the film, herself lists '*Allah tero naam*', the bhajan sung by Nanda on screen, as among her favourites. Playing close to his master's modus operandi, Jaidev used the voices of Lata, Asha and Rafi for a range of melodious compositions – romantic ditties to ghazals to bhajans – to create a name for himself, and a place for his music in cinema history.

None of which would have happened if S.D. Burman had not freed the junior composer from his leash.

49

I look at the man, and I am sad. Guru has been a friend, and admirer. How he used to leave everything and come running to listen to my new tune the moment he learnt I had composed something new.

But now, the same boyish smile is replaced by a frown. He frowns strangely, unlike anyone I know, his brow furrows both upwards and across his face. It perhaps indicates a man who thinks and worries at many levels.

Two brilliant personalities, Geeta and Guru – I sigh when I think about how their lives have been rocked. Whose fault is it when something goes wrong in a marriage? When two people who have decided they are with each other for life, suddenly have nothing to say to each other that does not hurt or wound?

I look at Meera, my staunch, loyal, and constant companion, and thank the Goddess for her steadfast love. I return it completely. After my music, it is my family I care about. They know it too.

Guru has come to me, he has a new film on the floors. After *Pyaasa*, he wants me to make the music for this film too.

Kaagaz Ke Phool: paper flowers. I look at the man sitting in the next room, as I confer with Meera, and think the name symbolizes him. His eyes have a haunted look, his brow is knit. Where is the debonair boy I knew? The simple ready-to-laugh creator of films? I hope he is not lost forever.

I am wondering how to work out the songs. Sahir is out of the question. He will insist on charging one rupee more, I will not agree, our paths may never cross again. He goes his way, I go mine. It makes me sad too, but I also have my pride. And my music is not any less creative. My life's blood is poured into my songs.

Guru Dutt wants Kaifi Azmi for the film. I'm in favour, I have said. Kaifi is a poet, a serious one, but the theme of the film is also serious.

I personally think Guru should make a happy, light film, it will ease his mood, make him smile again. Untangle some aspects of his life. But he is knitting it all the tighter, with Waheeda as his heroine, and Geeta singing the songs.

Geeta is a fine artiste, I think I can make her forget her misery through song. And Guru will also forget his sorrows in the making of his film.

I hear he is looking to film it in cinemascope; he wants to make news by using the new technology. I don't know if it will work, but he is gifted, and knows what he is doing.

I of course will do what I know best, make the music for the scenes.

Though the film is intended to be very serious, the characters are so too, I must find a way to introduce some lightness in the songs. Or who will watch the film?

50

Kaifi rose to the challenge. The song, '*Ek do teen char aur panch*', sung by Geeta and a chorus and shot on Waheeda and the children in the film, proved to be a popular aid to teach basic numbers in schools, for a brief period.

The simplicity of tune and the easy juxtaposition of a hierarchy in the numbers in the words, made it both endearing and complex enough to hold meaning for teacher and student alike.

However, history reports that the film, hailed as a classic now, failed miserably at the box office. Analysing the cause, Abrar Alvi, assistant to Guru Dutt, opined that it could be that at a time when food and shelter were basic preoccupations of the masses, a film that portrayed the internal emotional struggle of a creative mind which had life's daily needs well taken care of, could not appeal or be understood by viewers. They chose to envy rather than sympathize. In other words, Guru Dutt's partly autobiographical film was well ahead of its time when it hit the screens at the turn of the 1960s.

Of all the wonderful songs composed for the film, the most enduring one visually and otherwise is the Geeta Dutt number, which almost echoed her own life situation: '*Waqt ne kiya*.'

The pathos of the rendering, the tune that almost defies metre only to adhere to it, and the innovative filming that used lighting and the fact that the two protagonists were not mouthing the lyrics, which was a first in Hindi cinema, made the song ageless and a classic.

In his book *Incomparable S.D. Burman*, H.Q. Chowdhury recounts a trying moment in the composition of the song. The onus was on poet Kaifi Azmi:

> Dada played a tune that everyone liked. But there was no situation in the film for it. Guru Dutt was adamant. We must create a situation. So Kaifi stated writing and gave several versions. But Guru Dutt did not like any and finally said, Ï can't help you because I don't have a situation for the song. It is best we leave it for now and keep the tune for another film.

To Kaifi it was like conceding defeat. He gave it another try and wrote '*Waqt ne kiya, kya haseen situm*'. Guru Dutt was happy, and it became the opening musical refrain of the film, repeated throughout the film.

SD was also instrumental in creating another masterpiece that students of Indian cinema take frequent recourse to. By making Rafi sing in his complete range of octaves, from soft and musing to declamatory and anguished in '*Dekhi zamane ki yaari*', the maestro combined with the lyricist and the director to create one of cinema's most memorable scenes. Coming as it does at the climax of *Kagaaz Ke Phool*, the song's sombre message and tone are underlined by the deep shadows that hide the protagonist as he moves towards the film's last shot. It is an image that lingers in the mind, and the song brings it to life every time one who has seen the film hears it played. A perfect blending of diverse creative talents towards a powerful statement.

51

Two stories are worth the telling about the 1960 film, *Bombai Ka Babu*.

Directed by Guru Dutt's former assistant, Raj Khosla, the film would star Suchitra Sen, Bengal's unparalleled heartthrob, with Bombay's own Dev Anand.

Bombai Ka Babu's storyline was not an open-and-shut love story. A thriller, which was Raj Khosla's favourite genre (*CID*, *Kala Pani* and later *Woh Kaun Thi*), it was written by Rajinder Singh Bedi and bore a slight resemblance to an O. Henry story titled 'The Double-Dyed Deceiver'.

However, the film ended up making the audience shift uneasily in their seats thanks to the hint of an incestuous relationship between the lead pair. That the issue was resolved without serious lapse did not help in any way.

The songs of the film, composed by S.D. Burman and written by Majrooh, however, ring out till this day.

Bombai Ka Babu was one of the few occasions when S.D. Burman took recourse to Mukesh's voice. He got him to sing the haunting and tear-jerking bidai geet, '*Chal re sajni*', almost against his own judgement. The song, however, proved to be a winner, and he was vindicated in his choice.

But it is the chorus song that Suchitra Sen sings with her 'sakhis' that holds a more interesting tale. The song had just a few years ago been filmed on Waheeda Rehman.

The film, a Telugu movie titled *Rojulu Marayi*, gave the actress her debut role as a dancer. A four-minute song that won the dancer Waheeda Rehman great popularity in Andhra Pradesh and especially in Hyderabad; it would also be her passport to Hindi cinema. By chance, Guru Dutt and his two assistants would meet her, watch the film clip in Hyderabad, and remember that the dancer was good enough to be signed on for a vamp's role in two of the films under production: *Pyaasa* and *CID*.

But it is the song that has a story too.

Based on a Telugu folk tune, the song, '*Eeruvaka sagaroo rannoo chinnananna*' caught the fancy of S.D. Burman, who loved its folksiness and the way it was different from the folk tunes of his own Bengal.

The composer asked Waheeda to sing the song. Waheeda, that Telugu song of yours, could you sing it for me?

Why, Dada, Waheeda asked, I am hardly a singer.

Tch, oh ho, I will not record your voice, I just want to hear it, Dada Burman responded.

Why, Dada, the actress asked again.

I liked the opening tune so much, I want to use it in my film, *Bombai Ka Babu*, he replied. It is from Andhra, a Telugu folk tune, and I like it very much, I shall use the opening bars for my song.

Waheeda was amazed. Usually, Dada, she said, tunes from Hindi are copied in the south…

No, no, Dada Burman responded, cutting her short, sing it to me, let me hear it.

Then, says Waheeda, I sang it in my tuneless voice and he used the tune exactly as it was, in his song for *Bambai Ka Babu*, with the words '*Dekhne mein bhola hai, dil ka salona, Bambai se aaya hai babu chinnananna*'.

52

All morning, Meera has been busy, moving in and out of rooms like a treadle through the loom. She won't stop to talk to me, her brow is knit with the many chores she wishes to finish, the sweets to be made, the gods to be washed and dressed in new clothes, the prayers to be said. It is a lot of fuss, but mothers like to fuss, I think. I, father, am sitting by the window, letting the air touch my face, blowing in from the fragrant champa tree outside, watching and knowing that the big moment is here.

So many things happen in mysterious ways. I know this boy of mine is rich in talent. He is a prince too, in his own right in the world of music. Have I not nurtured him, and stoked his pride in his work over the years? Right from the time he played the tabla, hitting the tight hide with plump fingers still loaded with baby fat, to his tune that I used for the topi song in *Funtoosh*!

I think the very fact that he is now called Pancham by one and all makes him turn to music as instinctively as the sunflower turns to the sun. I am proud of the fact, my chest heaves with pride, my eyes shine with a sudden dazzle, but I hide it well. It does not do to praise a boy too much. Let the world praise him first.

I think the name of the film is so apt. *Chhote Nawab*. I have watched him toil over the music, his frown like his mother's, his lips pursed in a way that reminds me of Dada … Yet he is different from us all. An individual in his own right, I think. Is there a rebel in him?

I listened with grave demeanour when he played the first notes of the song he wants to record.

Surprised that it was classical. A soft, haunting tune. Why did I imagine he was a rebel? Or is he hiding it for now, walking cautiously with his first film, his debut in the world where his father along with others holds sway. Will he break free and be his own person once he gains a foothold of recognition?

Only time will tell.

Meera rebukes me, without saying a word. Pancham is going to record his first song, and you are just sitting by the window. That is what her look says, as she sweeps past me into the kitchen. Ah, Meera, my dear wife, if you only knew what I have done for our son!

I have crossed the desert and sipped the wine of reconciliation. I picked up the phone this morning. And even as you were in the kitchen, rattling pots and pans in preparation to appease the gods, I appeased the anger that had driven Lata and me apart. My son is recording for his first film, and Lata must sing … will you sing for him, I asked.

And the nightingale whose voice my music has not touched for so long, sweetly agreed. She will sing for Pancham. How could she not, the boy has grown up under her gaze.

In such moments are great decisions made, true relationships restored. Though I have had voices as good, I think Krishna's flute plays in Lata's voice. In her my songs find solace. I am happy. Sure now we will work together again.

53

There are many versions of the rift between the composer and his favourite singer, the causes, the mending. Suffice it to say here that whichever of them is the right version, the fact remains that the rift hurt both parties equally. On his part, S.D. Burman–even though he played tic-tac-toe with the many voices available to him, choosing one over the other to suit the mood and metre of his song–felt Lata was crucial to his music. 'Give me a harmonium, a tabla and give me Lata, and I will give you memorable songs,' or words to that effect have gone on record as reported by Ritu Chandra in the S.D. Burman Birth Centenary Commemorative Souvenir.

And indeed he did use the nightingale's voice in songs that brought every shade of emotion and feeling, from the plaintive to the sacred to the mischievous, even guiding her into a cabaret without letting her inbuilt hesitation about such songs hamper his resolve to have her voice the number.

On her part, Lata Mangeshkar, though she reigned supreme in the playback field, with sister Asha a close second, held the composer in utmost reverence. He was older, almost a father figure, someone for whom music was a deity, palpable and throbbing with life, and her voice a means to reach to that godhood. The rift was almost unbreachable as each held on to pride, but a father bows before a son's need, and an artiste before great music. By the time *Chhote Nawab* was recorded, Lata and S.D. Burman had bridged the gap that had held them apart and were putting in their best. Once again for an old familiar creative genius, Bimal Roy. The film: *Bandini*.

54

Mora gora ang lai le, mohe Shaam rang dai de
Chhup jaungi raat hi me, mohe pi ka sang dai de…

Bandini was epoch making in many ways. For one, it brought Lata back into S.D. Burman's studio, and started off a new era of melody-making where the nightingale would embellish Dada's tunes, making musical history along the way.

Just for the record, though Lata first sang for S.D. Burman again for *Bandini* after a six-year gap, it was her song '*Pavan deewani*' for the 1962 film *Dr Vidya*, tuned by SD and shot on a dancing Vyjayanthimala on screen, that sent the first signal that the great rift between singer and music composer was mended.

But to get back to *Bandini*. At another level, even as it mended one rift, the film resulted in another break, though thankfully for lovers of Hindi film music it did not go the way the Sahir–SD break had. This time, S.D. Burman fell out with Shailendra, the lyricist. Nothing Bimal-da said would appease Dada's anger; the maestro was adamant. He would not work with Shailendra.

It is the writer's magnanimity that rather than take offence and walk off in a huff, leaving the production to flounder for want of a lyricist, Shailendra put forward the name of a young man who worked as a car mechanic and slept in a shack while he dreamed of making a career in literature.

At a literary festival in Bhutan, Gulzar, proud possessor of an Oscar for his work, among other honours, spoke about how he was commissioned by S.D. Burman. And persuaded to write the song.

'Those days I used to work in a garage. My job was to mix the paint to touch up cars that had got damaged in an accident. I had met Shailendra because we were both members of a youth choir, the Bombay Youth Choir.'

Shailendra, as was the practice in those times, of one artiste helping another, had persuaded Gulzar to meet Bimal-da, who was shooting *Bandini* at that time. Bimal Roy's assistant, Debu Sen, aware of Gulzar's poetic abilities approached him when, thanks to the film's music director, *Bandini* was left without a songwriter. Gulzar was reluctant, and, but for Shailendra's persuasion would have never met Bimal Roy.

'I was not interested,' Gulzar recounted. 'I was more interested in literature, my first love, and did not want anything to do with films or songs. But Shailendra insisted.'

What followed was almost a scene from a comic film. Gulzar met Bimal Roy. Roy asked Debu in Bengali if the gentleman knew Bengali and, more importantly, Vaishnavi poetry, and could he write it?

Embarrassed, Debu whispered that Gulzar did, could and incidentally knew Bengali quite well. Gulzar says in an interview that he thought he saw Bimal-da blush!

One thing led to another. Sachin Dev Burman sat the poet down and made him listen to the tune he had composed. He was commissioned to write the words.

'It took no time for me to write the song, but a week to polish it,' says Gulzar, who even today spends more time polishing than in writing a poem.

The song, depicting the awakening of love and sexual passion in the mind of a naive village girl, Kalyani (Nutan), was set in a frame that suited all the players in *Bandini* perfectly.

The rusticity of the setting, the innocent expressiveness of Nutan, the moon shifting through the clouds to shine on a patch of water, the sound of crickets and the night breeze in the trees, were powerful aids to both the songwriter and the composer.

Gulzar penned the bhajan-esque love song with what would become his trademark style, bringing in literary and mythological allusions, as in Nutan's curse to the moon that rahu should overshadow it, as well as his powerful ability to draw word pictures. More important in the history of Hindi film lyrics, Gulzar brought in the use of complex word associations and usage, moving away from the simple lyricism of earlier poets. '*Mora gora ang lai le, mohe Shaam rang dai de*' was precursor to more intricate word association imagery.

Lata, as if to make up for the five-year separation from one of her favourite composers, gave the song her sweetest voice, and SD, perhaps inspired by the setting, so reminiscent of his childhood haunts, tuned the song to a melody that has kept it alive all these years.

Also on record is Gulzar's story about an awkward moment, when after he had written the song, the composer asked him if he could sing.

Gulzar admits that singing had never been one of his talents.

'Then you do not need to go to Bimal-da with the songs, I will explain them to him myself. Arre, tum kaisa bhi sunayega, aur mera tune reject ho jayega,' SD is reported to have said.

But of course Gulzar could not keep away, and tagged along, to see how his song would take musical shape!

S.D. Burman also had a small tiff with his Bimal-da over the picturization of the song. The director had planned it as an indoor shot, while the composer had created a tune that gathered the outdoors within its melody. Finally, the resolution came with the observation that it was simpler for a woman to go out singing into the night in a milieu known to her, than to sing of her love indoors where her father might possibly overhear!

In Gulzar's words:

> '*Mora goraa ang layi le*' – iss geet ka janam vahaan se shuroo huaa jab Bimal-da aur Sachin-da called me to explain the situation. Sachin-da stated: 'Kalyani has started getting involved romantically with Bikaash, but it's all in her mind still. One night, after winding up her chores in the kitchen, she hums as she comes out of the house…'
>
> 'Such a character cannot go out of the house and sing,' Bimal-da, stopped his flow abruptly.
>
> 'If she does not go out of the house, will she sing in front of her father?' Sachin-da retorted.
>
> 'She has always listened to Vaishnav poems from her father, why can't she sing to him?' Bimal-da responded.
>
> 'This is not a Vaishnav poem, Dada, it is a song,' Burman-da emphasized.

'So write a poem, she will sing a poem...'

'The song will be stifled inside the house...'

'Then get her into the courtyard. She won't go out...'

That settled it. Burman-da sat back. 'If she does not go out, I won't make the song,' he said.

So it went on. I heard the entire story from Debu. Bimal-da then called me again and explained the scene to me. 'It is night. She is afraid of stepping out, in case someone should see her in the moonlight, she is not able to go beyond the courtyard.'

Then Sachin-da sent for me. I explained Bimal-da's position. Sachin-da said, 'She is afraid someone will see her in the moonlight. So, she can come out from the courtyard and yet keep looking back.'

I started understanding the nuances of the scene now ... and poor Kalyani's predicament.

The next day, Sachin-da called and sang the tune to me. La-laa la-la-la la-la-la la-la-laa.

Pancham changed it a bit: Da-daa daa~daa daa~daa da-da-daa.

The song started revealing itself, some of it la la and some da da. I told myself, I am deaf to the sur and taal, and kept looking at both father and son, wanting so much to tell them I don't understand, so ta-ta-ta-ta.

Sachin-da kept playing the tune on his harmonium. I started humming it, and some broken words came to me to fit to the tune.

Do-chaar ... do chaar ... duyi-chaar pag pe anganaa
Bairee kangnaa chhanak na

Some words started being strung together:

> Bairee kangnaa chhanak na
> Duyi-chaar pag pe anganaa
> Mohe koson door laage…

Sachin-da sang in his very tuneful voice and checked the words out, and said, 'Yes, this is how the words should fit to the tune.'

I left. Kept humming and thinking of Kalyani. A thought presented itself to me: she will appeal to the moon–let me see my lover, turn your face away, O Moon. But the moon would filter through the clouds and look at her, smiling to himself, as if asking, where are you going? how will you go? I will fill the night with light, and everyone will see you. Kalyani, angered by this, curses the moon:

> Tohe raahu laage bairee
> Muskaaye jee jalaayi ke'

She sits down, thinking she should go back, but her love and desire pull her by the hand, making her wish to continue on her way; and her shyness holds her by the foot, stopping her. Not knowing what she should do, she asks herself:

> Kahaan le chalaa hai manavaa
> Mohe baanwaree banaayi ke.

Quiet and thoughtful, Kalyani sits, thinking to herself, if only there were no moonlight today, or if I were not quite so fair–I gleam in the moonlight. If I were dark,

I could go concealed in the darkness to meet my love.
She returns home, the poor girl, singing to herself:

> Mora goraa ang layi le
> Mohe Shaam rang dayi de
> Chhup jaaoongi raat hi mein
> Mohe pee ka sang dayi de

Characteristically, S.D. Burman patched up with Shailendra. Though impressed with Gulzar's poem for his song, he quickly set him aside for Shailendra, insisting the senior writer write the other songs for the film.

If Gulzar was hurt, he did not show it, realizing he was a stop-gap arrangement indeed.

However, Bimal Roy, embarrassed by the music maestro's move, and also impressed by the young poet's calibre, asked him to throw up the car mechanic's job and assist him in his next film, *Kabiluwala*.

♫

From a folder cover of Legends S.D. Burman: The Inimitable Composer, *VOLS 1-5, (RPG Music, STHV 132487/91), Subhash K. Jha writing in the booklet accompanying the* CD *set:*

The luscious arrangements of '*Mora gora ang lai le, mohe shaam rang dayi de*' has a looming history behind it. This is the song with which Sachin-da and his favourite 'Lota' patched up their differences. The incident bears testimony to the composers' temperamental genius. Lata-ji arrived at the Burmans' bungalow 'The Jet' to meet R.D. Burman who had decided to turn music director and wanted his father's favourite singer to sing his first song. No sooner did the nightingale arrive at the Burmans' residence than she inquired about the senior Burman from the junior. 'He is in the next room,' RD informed her; minutes later the cold war was over. 'How many of your singing dates can you give me,' Burman Dada stormed in. 'As many as you want,' replied the nightingale.

♫

Gulzar recalls how easily Sachin-da would get offended. 'Woh bachchon ki tarah rooth jaate,' the poet-lyricist says, laughing.

It is this purity and innocence of a child that comes gushing to the surface in the compositions of S.D. Burman. Not calculated for applause, his tunes are timeless by dint of their guileless beauty.

Another consequence of Gulzar working on the lyrics for S.D. Burman in *Bandini* was the fact that he met Pancham for the first time. The meeting would culminate in a friendship that would create great work by combining the lyrics of Gulzar with the tunes of R.D. Burman, and as in the case of their non-film collection *Dil Padosi Hai*, use the versatility of Asha Bhonsle to showcase the incomparable results of the combination of two musical giants.

Bandini also marked the coming of age of Asha Bhonsle as a singer.

Working with S.D. Burman, as he had fallen out with her elder sister, Asha had over the six years honed her voice to be teasing, sensual, melodious by turn. Asha was his replacement for a Geeta Dutt whose personal life was in too much of a mess to allow her to sing the way she wanted, or present herself at rehearsals the way S.D. Burman expected of all his singers.

In earlier films like *Chalti Ka Naam Gaadi* and *Nau Do Gyarah*, Asha, often paired with an equally light-as-air Kishore Kumar, had teased her way into listeners' hearts, with songs that were ebullient.

In *Bandini*, S.D. Burman gave her a new identity. Just as he had worked with Geeta to change her image from soulful to sexy, the teasing, flirtatious tenor of Asha's voice was shaded with pathos with a single number in *Bandini*. As the voice of the woman serving a life sentence who longs for her days of childhood and messages from home, Asha sang '*Ab ke baras*' with such grace and feeling that it moved many to tears long after the scene was forgotten.

In interviews given much later, Asha goes on record to acknowledge her debt to her composer, explaining that his trick of adding an exclamation before a line, or an inflection to show a mood was something she treasured. He also told her how to use her breath to advantage in fade-ins and fadeouts, so the intake and expulsion of air from the lungs was almost unnoticeable.

Asha said in an interview to *Filmfare* in 1965: 'I consider him my guru, he taught me the importance of feelings, when you sing for a particular role, you must feel you are that person. So, whether I am singing a qawwali or a cabaret, I try to identify myself with the character.'

S.D. Burman, on his part, held the singer he had helped shape, and who added to her repertoire nuances she had learnt from O.P. Nayyar, in high esteem.

In the same *Filmfare* interview, Asha adds: 'He used to tell me, "There are thumris and ghazals, but you are my tarana, tar-tar-tar karti rehti ho,"' alluding to her habit of walking around his house wearing paijans that sounded loudly with every step.

55

1963!

He stared at the calendar on the wall; the breeze played tricks with the pages, now revealing one month, now another, sometimes the top of March teamed with the bottom of August, or May.

Like life, he thought, good, bad, past, present, all mixed up in the memory.

The pain had subsided, his eye was still swathed in bandages, the gauze feeling like a dead weight on his eyelid and making his brow hot, but the pain, thankfully, was dull.

Not so the pain that sat like a stone on his heart.

No, he told himself firmly, you will not walk that path again. It is not like you.

True, he mused to himself, his one open eye still watching the flying pages of the calendar jumbling up past, present and future. True that he did not believe in accolades, or awards, or recognition of any kind. They were transitory, hollow. They reflected the whims of those in power.

But he had to admit he had been pleased. 'You look like a child who has just been given the moon, what is it?' Meera had cried out, when she saw him holding the receiver of the phone over which he had heard the news that he had been given an award by the Sangeet Natak Academy for his music in films, though he knew the real spur had been his songs in *Pyaasa*.

Even Pancham had been over the moon with delight. 'I will also win such an award,' the boy had cried as he did a little impromptu tabla piece on the table to express his joy.

It had been a singular honour, and he had not been able to pretend he was not touched or impressed.

Guru had also been so happy, he was surely the most unselfish of men, he thought.

Why does this hurt? he thought. Am I changing?

He had poured his soul out for his films, for *Bandini*, for *Meri Surat Teri Ankhen*. Crafted each song with the care of god fashioning a human being.

Bandini, he learnt, had won awards, many of them. Bimal-da would be pleased, he was himself pleased for Bimal-da. But his music had found no place, not a mention.

And today, this afternoon, he could not bring himself to look at Manna's face.

The boy sat at his feet, near his bed, asking how he was.

He knew Manna's heart was bleeding, he always knew such things. Something tied his heart to the boy's. 'Don't call him a boy,' Meera had once admonished him, hearing him refer to Manna in that manner. 'He's a grown man now.'

'But to me he is always a child, the nephew of my guru,' he had replied.

To Manna he gave the songs that he felt were priceless gems that only his voice could reveal the purity of.

Like the song in *Manzil*, '*Hato kaheko jhuti banao batiyan*', based on the bandish of no less a singer than Ustad Faiyaz

Khan. He had crafted it to appeal to the filmgoer's taste, and handed it like a precious burden to Manna, admonishing him to sing it with care. It was, after all, the bandish of a great singer.

And in a film that had every voice that was popular in it, from Rafi to Hemant to Manna all singing for Dev, the hero, it had been Manna who had won the day. With a song shot on not the hero but the comedian, Mehmood. Mehmood had added his virtuoso treatment to the song on film, to make it hold its own alongside the film's other popular numbers '*Dil to diwana hai*' and '*Yaad aa gayi wo nashili nigahen*'.

He smiled at the thought that a classical song should cross the barrier to popularity so easily. It was all Manna's genius that made it happen. His deft use of voice, his knowledge of the raga. But despite its popularity, the song had not even been nominated!

Of course, he himself never looked at lists and nominations, but somehow he was sure that Manna would win the best singer this year at least. For *Meri Surat Teri Aankhen*...

The way he had sung that difficult song, '*Poochho na maine kaise rain bitaye*', in one single take! Faultless, emotion filling the voice with perfection, emotion taking the voice effortlessly from one note to the other, delineating the raga with virtuosity and ease.

He smiled ... how Jaidev had come rushing out of the recording room to take Manna's hand, telling him the song was pure music sung divinely. Manna had turned red with the effort, or perhaps the compliment.

He himself had been more moderate. That had always been his style. No singer or composer was greater for him than the song itself. No lyricist either. There was always in a song that untouched pinnacle of perfection that no singer except Saraswati herself could hope to reach!

He had stayed almost silent that day, offering only a modest compliment, but even Manna had understood that he was pleased.

And that might have fanned his hope of an award.

Then, to know that the song and the singer had not won!

Ah well, it is all about popularity, he told himself, stopping with a prudent thought the tear that welled up unbidden in his seeing eye. The film had not gone wonderfully well with the masses. Only its songs had reverberated from radios on and off.

But the pang he felt would not be stilled. It mocked at him, a hook pulling against his heart, telling him that somewhere he must realize that everyone was not quite the saint he was, that Manna must have had dreams, which were so rudely smashed.

He should have been more discreet, asked someone else instead of Manna, but he had blurted out, 'Did you get it?' Only to hear silence in response. 'Tu bolta kyon nahin,' he cried, and Manna answered, softly, 'Not just I but the entire film industry thought you would get the award for this film.' Thinking not of his loss, but mine, what a soul he is, he thought to himself in admiration; but grief welled up all the same.

'Was it possible for anyone to sing better?' he had cried, anguish flooding his throat.

The truth lay elsewhere. In mass appeal, in other voices also adept at expression, in being heard more often than the lone voice of a classical composition in a film that half-flopped in the box office stakes.

Manna's time would come. Awards or otherwise, he would prove to the world that he was of the finest metal, a true nephew and student of the unmatchable K.C. Dey. And he, Sachin Dev Burman of Tripura, would ensure that it would happen.

One fallout of *Manzil* was that Manna came to be regarded as Mehmood's voice. He would sing innumerable songs for the comedian, including the classical duet with Geeta in *Ziddi*, '*Main tere pyaar mein kya kya na bana dilbar*', and the inimitable duet with Kishore in *Padosan*, '*Ek chatur naar*', the former tuned by S.D. Burman, the latter by son, RD.

In fact, *Meri Surat Teri Aankhen* was the high point of S.D. Burman's experimentation with giving the classical song a popular form.

In his own words, from *Sargamer Nikhad*, a story on the other classical number, by Rafi, '*Naache mann mora*':

> I carried out a similar experiment in *Meri Surat Teri Ankhen*. Shailendra wrote a song starting with '*Naache mann mora, magan tigda dhigi dhigi*'. The idea for the song occurred to me this way. Sri Bindadin Maharaj, the famous Kathak artist, while teaching dance to his nephews always chanted the phrase 'tigda dhigi dhigi' and according to this instructed the foot stances. I shared a very cordial relation with Achhan Maharaj and this phrase was imprinted in my mind. Using my tune, I helped Shailendra to write this song. I proposed the first line as, 'The mind is dancing, or the mind is dancing like a peacock, or such a similar lyric. He wrote, '*Naache man mora magan*'; after which I used

> the phrase 'tigda dhigi dhigi'. For the expression, proper rhythm was used in the tune. Pandit Samta Prasad from Benaras played tabla for this number. He was invited specially to play according to the Kathak dance phrases. Everybody liked this composition.

U.K. Dubey recounts how he was called to play the dholak for '*Poochho na kaise*'. He and many other musicians sat quiet, while the song was being recorded

> There were ten of us. Pancham and Maruti had booked us for the song–four dholak, two tabla players, and four side rhythm players. Dada came in and took a long look. We were of course busy rehearsing, practising our bits. He said, no-no, and called Maruti aside, saying, 'I don't want anyone, just that one tabla, bas!"
>
> And the recording was ready to start.
>
> We sat there quietly. The Union rule was that if an artiste is called and reaches the studio for a recording, he must be paid. So we sat, waiting to take our money after the recording was done.
>
> Dada was not around at the time of booking, Pancham and Maruti decided there should be ten rhythm players and ten others, so there was a crowd of twenty!
>
> But Dada started recording with just one tabla, and the other instruments, and completed the song in one take!
>
> That was how he worked.

♫

Perhaps no other year demonstrates the versatility of the composer as well as the year he created the music for *Meri Surat Teri Aankhen* – 1963.

Walking in step with this film was *Tere Ghar Ke Samne*, frothy, light, a love story with fun, feud and a predictable happy ending – vintage Navketan. However, *Tere Ghar Ke Samne* was not given the reception that S.D. Burman probably expected – though the songs endure to this day. In spite of the fact that he tuned numbers as varied and remarkable as the breezy '*Dil ka bhawar kare pukar*', and the moonlight-drenched romantic '*Tu kahan yeh bata*', both sung by Rafi and picturized on Dev in different moods, the critics called the songs the creations of an ageing composer.

An aside: Singing star Suraiya, who never got over her love for Dev Anand, went on record to say that of all the songs on Dev, she thought '*Tu kahan yeh bata*', which she counted among Rafi's best, was her favourite.

The critics were proved wrong soon enough. S.D. Burman followed up with a breakaway music theme for his first Muslim social, *Benazir*, with at least two songs that are still hummed. One, the Rafi number, '*Dil mein ek jaane tamanna*' and, two, Lata's '*Alvida jaane wafa*'. SD's varied classical training that included influences from the northern Muslim gharanas must have played a role in shaping the music of Benazir, effortlessly.

S.D. Burman followed up with *Kaise Kahoon*, another film that had songs with a classical base. Though the film went nowhere, its Suman Kalyanpur-Rafi number '*Manmohan man mein*' would win for SD a singular honour, the Swami Haridas Award for best classical song.

56

Sorrow coils about me, slithering in unexpected. I have heard disturbing news.

They have pulled down Mantri Bari. Demolished a structure my father built, used, walked through with his long striding steps. He will walk there no more; there is only rubble and ruin where the house once stood. The government works in strange ways. They will build now where they have demolished. Another structure. For another great man, Rabindranath. The Rabindra Bhavan will be dedicated to the great poet.

Why destroy to build? We could have shared the space; they could have shared the space that existed, my father and the poet. Neither would have minded it. In fact, they would have enjoyed being under the same roof, if only notionally.

History is destroyed thus, by wanton thoughts of officials.

I feel my father is gone further into the hazy mists of lost time.

57

I watch you, Meera, as you sleep. There are soft lines on your face, how I have not noticed them before, I don't know. Maybe when you are awake, and animated, they are erased by the movement of your eyes.

Time has etched its passing on you gently, but you are in so many ways, a gentle soul.

Though beneath the silk, there is iron, as firm and strong as the bangle on your wrist.

I look at you and think of the faces that have crossed my life, our lives. The faces I have written songs for.

How different each has been from the other.

You remember the time we went to watch *Kala Pani*? How we had wondered at Madhubala's expressions, her ability to create a mood with one flick of her eyes or a twist of a smile?

The songs I have created on women, on their looks, their beauty. The poets have written their hearts out, sometimes creating the beauty with their words. When there are words that tell a woman she is beautiful, she must feel that way, and it surely helps her look more beautiful.

Nutan, Waheeda Rehman, Asha Parekh, Sharmila Tagore, and then, Kalpana Kartik, Shakila, Vyjayanthimala, Tanuja.

What faces, what actresses. And what songs they have sung on screen. And have had sung about them. A lifetime of emotion.

Yet, when I watch you asleep, the sweat shining on your face, the eyes quivering ever so softly as you dream perhaps, I see in you the essence of all those songs.

You alone are my strength, my support. And I hope in my search for the soul of music I have not left you alone too often. If so, forgive me, Meera. But my music is a goddess I cannot refuse. She is my Radha.

You, my Meera.

And yet, my soul lives in you!

58

Has anyone ever wondered why S.D. Burman, blessed with two talented artistes in his own home, never really gave them full rein? Pancham was always a son, a learner; at least that is how his father saw him. Chief assistant, accompanist, arranger, who he knew was talented, who had composed songs that SD had adapted. The *Funtoosh* song, '*Aye meri topi palat ke aa*', being one example. But never really under his baton did RD get full freedom to compose a complete song; it was also unlikely that he would be given the credit for composing a tune on his father's behalf, if such a thing ever did come to pass.

It happens often that sons remain sons, and till they fly out to show they have grown and can find their own creative space, the shadow of the parent covers their genius.

But it is Meera's status that is less understandable. Meera was trained, her voice was clear, her understanding of music complete, later in life she would take on the arranging of S.D. Burman's music. It was Meera who helped preserve her husband's compositions by weaving them together as notations. She composed the lyrics for many of the Bangla songs SD sang, proving she understood the qualities of his voice truly too. Her compositions were close to the soil, in content and expression.

Sudipta Chandra, in a feature in *The Statesman* published in April 2010 narrates the story first narrated by Brojen Biswas, who played the tabla for many of S.D. Burman's compositions and in fact taught R.D. Burman tabla.

> Karta, Meera-di and myself were visiting a village in what today is Bangladesh. We found a little girl who was recently married. She was sitting on the river bank, weeping loudly. I asked her the reason. She replied she had recently got married and was waiting for her brother. But he didn't show up. The moment had an

> intense impact on Meera's mind. She came out with the classic *'Ke jaash re bhaati gang baaiya'* which SD composed the tune for and sang. The song has undergone many renderings since.

More important, Meera understood her husband's creative genius perfectly, understood every nuance of his compositions, could even train the singers into perfect rendition. Listen to her singing *'Kali badariyan chha gayi'* as early as in 1948, a duet she recorded with her Karta, and the voice is clear, the melody perfect and the song rings true. Meera recorded songs with SD till as late as 1949; most of them in Bangla.

Why then, when she had in past years proved a perfect foil to her husband's voice in duets both in Bangla and in Hindi, her diction clear and unaccented, was she never a voice used for film by SD? Was it a classic case of not seeing a gem so close to the home due to creative shortsightedness? Or a question of market preferences.

Though, as records clearly so, SD was not one to bow to market preferences. He decided which voice should sing his song, at every turn.

Perhaps, in a life blameless and pure in the pursuit of music, this is the one cause for censure. That Meera never gave her voice to cinema, under her husband's or any other baton. That he who had suffered the same neglect, only to rise above it, did not use the lesson thus learnt to lift his singer wife above being just a wife and an assistant!

♫

From the Foreword by Salil Ghosh in S.D. Burman's autobiography Sargamer Nikhad

Before you start reading Sachin-da's story in his own words, I want to say something about Meera Boudi. Meera Devi's inspiration, encouragement and company has been an integral part of Sachin-da's successful music career. Meera Boudi has not only been a wife, but simultaneously she has also been Sachin-da's representative, manager, and music writer too. Boudi herself is musically accomplished and a good singer too. One day I asked Sachin-da, 'Doesn't Boudi sing ? I want to organize a solo performance by her.'

Sachin Karta smiled and replied, 'Where does Meera get the time to practice music? Her time goes in keeping track of my income tax.'

It is true. Sachin-da's single-minded pursuit of music for thirty years without any distraction has been possible only because of Meera Devi. Shouldering all of Sachin-da's responsibilities, Meera Devi has been managing everything wonderfully.

59

Guide is remembered for many things. Mainly its music, which moves even a generation that has not watched the film.

Guide brought to a head the power of S.D. Burman the singer.

The very first song and almost the last one are sung in his inimitable nasal, rasping yet amazingly melodious voice.

'*Wahan kaun hai tera*', filmed on an emotionally lost and

socially outcast Dev Anand at the start of *Guide*, set the tone of the film. Here was the start of a film from the end of a long journey undertaken by a man who would move through many lives in the course of a few hours on screen. *'Allah megh de paani de'*, based on a classic Bengali folk song, in the composer's voice with a chorus joining in, brings the film full circle, musically as well as a narrative.

In many ways, *Guide* was the encapsulation of an entire life. The songs were the milestones marking distinct turning points.

Created and sung in the Bhatiali vein that underlined the philosophy closest to the composer's own heart, the opening song is almost symbolic of S.D. Burman's own life and career as composer. The heart attack that had struck him a few years ago without warning must have held up a mirror to life in the unsteady world he now belonged to – where one was cherished and feted as long as one stood firm at the pinnacle, and could easily be passed over at the first stumble.

There is no real record of his pain, but the composer, who held two people in great esteem, must have felt the ground shift under his feet when one of them turned away, seeking a new partner for his latest venture rather than wait for his favourite to recover.

But history shows that Guru Dutt was always a man in a hurry, impatient to keep the unit occupied, anxious to move to a new production even as the old one was done. He could not wait for S.D. Burman, who would take at least three months to recover fully, if he would recover enough at all to make music again. Guru Dutt, with the same swiftness of decision and uncompromising attitude that the composer showed towards his singers when it came to his own creations, moved swiftly to another old partner, O.P. Nayyar, for his next film.

In an interview given to *Filmfare* in 1984, R.D. Burman spoke of the troubled time:

> That the film industry is full of fair-weather friends I came to know in 1961 when my father had a heart attack. At that time he had already composed about five songs for Guru Dutt's *Baharen Phir Bhi Aayengi*. My parents told Guru Dutt that I was capable of getting the songs recorded but he declined and said sorry but he couldn't wait. After that one by one all the producers left my father. The only one to stick with him was Dev Anand–he told my father not to worry, that he'd delay the film. That's something nobody will ever do for a music director today. Five months later, when my father had recovered, we finished all the *Guide* songs in five days and will you believe it, at the first session, Dev Anand okayed four tunes? Shailendra even penned three songs right there: '*Aaj phir jeene ki tamanna hai*', '*Din dhal jaaye*' and '*Tere mere sapne*'.

Dard se tera koi na tadpa / Aankh kiski na roi–did SD think of himself when he sang the words? Perhaps. But he was not one to dwell on such thoughts.

To his credit, Dev Anand, the other producer and actor closest to S.D. Burman, stayed true. He would wait for the composer to come back and swing his baton. The music of *Guide* would wait.

Despite S.D. Burman's own entreaties to Dev Anand that

he be replaced, the producer of *Guide* was adamant. It was S.D. Burman or nothing. If the composer could not make other songs, he would run the film with the one song he had composed before he fell ill. In fact, Dev Anand refused to even have the song recorded in Dada Burman's absence. '"No, Dada, this song will not be recorded until the time you recover from your illness. It can only be done by you." And we waited for three months. And the song was "*Gaata rahe mera dil*",' he said in an interview on CNN/IBN in a programme on S.D. Burman.

Perhaps, it was all for the composer's good, that he was left with only *Guide* to work on, on his recovery.

Even as Shailendra, who was back working with S.D. Burman again, and was his announced favourite among lyricists, wrote '*Aaj phir jeene ki tamana hai*', S.D. Burman swung back to his creative mode, drinking deep of the fount he knew best. Music. It was a second life, and he would live it to the full! Thus, the exuberant strains of '*Gaata rahe mera dil*', a celebration of love in the film, but S.D. Burman's personal celebration of life.

Guide saw some of the best talents in the field coming together with the composer to create a score that has no downs. Every song was perfection, fitted aptly to the scene, sung with passion and fervour. Every song a polished gem of composition, words and setting.

Classical wizards like Hari Prasad Chaurasia, Shiv Kumar Sharma, steady arrangers and accompanists like Suhrid Kaur and Manohari, as well as his favourite voices, Lata Mangeshkar, Kishore Kumar and Mohammad Rafi would work together to create magic for the film that would place S.D. Burman back in the forefront of Indian film music composers.

SD took on the task with his usual dedication and seemed to have bounced back with vigour. His creative juices were flowing freely again; the rest had been a blessing in disguise, a respite from the daily demands of composing.

But perhaps his mind had not been still for a moment. After all, this was a composer who had never needed the crutch of a harmonium to start the tune unfolding. It would unravel at any time, at strange moments of peace, or in the strangest of places. Was not '*Jaayen to jaayen kahan*' composed when he had lost his way during a walk? And '*Yeh raat, yeh chandni*' appear to him almost complete while he stared at the moonlit expanse outside his window? His tunes were drawn from the sights and sounds around him. The twitter of birds, the flash movement of squirrel, they had musical meaning for him.

Chances are the ceiling of the ward he was interred at was enough of an inspiration!

60

Composing and recording the music for *Guide*, S.D. Burman would spring a few surprises.

Here, from an interview by Moti Lalwani and Richa Lakhanpal with santoor wizard Pandit Shiv Kumar Sharma, is an incident:

> I used to also play the tabla, and it is a little-known fact that in the song '*Mose chhal kiye jaaye*' I was the accompanist on the tabla. I used to play the tabla professionally but by that time, I had stopped playing.

But, we were friends, Pancham and I. If I was present during a music sitting, and there was a tabla nearby, I would pick it up and start playing. In those days, '*Mose chhal kiye jaaye*' was being composed for *Guide*. Maruti Rao Keer was the regular accompanist on tabla for Dada. I was keeping the rhythm on tabla, when Dada said, 'You will play the tabla.'

I said, 'But I have stopped playing … I don't play the tabla…'

But Dada said, 'No, no, just play. I want you to play for this song.'

Pancham and Dada just got after me then. That was the only song for *Guide* I accompanied on the tabla, and the only song ever, after I had stopped playing the tabla. I never did it for any other music director, but could not refuse Dada. Of course I played the santoor for most of his other compositions.

61

I should not be afraid any more, he told himself, but even as the set was being prepared, his heart skipped a beat.

True, he was a well-known music director, almost everybody revered him and called him Dada, but it could be my age, he mused, not because they think the world of my compositions.

He remembered with a pang that his song, among the best he had composed till date, '*Poochho na kaise*' had not won any awards; was he then really good enough?

But awards are … oof, he told himself, shaking away the thought.

There was work at hand. The real test would begin now.

Waheeda had listened to the music; he could not quite make out what her face said, but she had listened intently. It was a tough scene, and she was to be the focus. He knew she was a good dancer, had watched her in other films, and she was a fast learner. The choreographer Sohanlal had been working on the scene too, and they had had some meetings, he knew that.

He on his part had told her what his music meant to express.

Anger, freedom, competition, sorrow ... an entire gamut of emotions felt by the heroine Rosie. If he had understood Goldie correctly, this was Rosie's moment of coming face to face with the life she lived. The segment had to mirror her frustration.

His main worry was the lack of words. Would a composition hold without words in a movie? Would the audience look at a dance that had no words?

He had used more instruments than he usually did; five rhythm instruments, the tabla, dholak, big dhol, chenda and the dafli, to create the base for the dance steps. He had layered them, alternating them in the segments, to change tempo and mood. The dance would need enough percussion support, and the ghungroo, the jharjari, kabbas and reso reso would provide that.

The clavioline stood in for the 'been'. Hemant Kumar had done it earlier in *Nagin* and it had worked so wonderfully then too. He added the melody in, layering in with the sitar, the banjo and the mandolin, and alternating them with solos on the sitar and tabla. That was more instruments than he normally used, but he knew here, in this piece, there was no singer and thus no danger of voice and words being drowned out. The music had to be complex, mesmerizing, and it had to suit the complex mood of the dancer and her execution of her emotions.

He was proud of the fact that his team had been wonderful, they had played like never before. 'Look,' he had told them, 'this composition has no words, only music, this is your chance to show your skill.' And they had played so beautifully.

He was pleased. But would the audience…

He watched as the filming began.

Waheeda in a black and red sari, a junior dancer in some village dress. But the camera rolled and he knew it would be focusing on Waheeda.

He watched as she danced, smiling first, enjoying the freedom to express with her body. Graceful, sinuous in keeping with the sound. Moving slowly into more intense body language, step after step, her face, and body, reflecting the music. She's reading the words in my music, he thought, surprised. She is bringing it to life. Saying everything so clearly.

The pace changed, and he could see anger, desperation. She is filling it with emotion, he thought.

And suddenly, even as he watched on, entranced, it was done. Cut, the director shouted, and the last take was complete!

He was beside himself, his confidence flooding back.

He was among geniuses. The choreographer, the dancer, the director, they all added their bit, and he was happy with what they had made of his composition.

People won't forget this snake dance anytime soon, he thought, smiling as he stepped out to meet Waheeda.

She was sweating a lot, the breath still rising fast in her chest, from the exertion and excitement of dancing. He felt humble before her talent, her dedication. She was not Waheeda then; in front of the camera, she had been Rosie!

Everyone had applauded.

As quoted in CNN-IBN Revisits the Musical Journey of S.D. Burman. *Remembering S.D. Burman*, Saturday, 12 November 2011: 'When I did this music, I thought without any song, any lyrics, no words, how to express her frustration. Waheeda maine socha nahin tha ki aise hoga. Mujhe to bahut darr tha, magar lagta hai tumhara gussa, tumhara dukh, sab kuch usmein nikal aaya.' In these words were encapsulated his thanks and his joy!

Waheeda's quote about the scene is also worth noting: 'Yes, being a classical dancer helped me to do those dances with the direction of late Hiralal and Sohanlal. The character wants to become a great dancer, very famous and very popular, and the music helped bring out the moves very nicely.'

Music arranger U.K. Dubey, who provided the list of instruments used in the snake dance, adds the interesting possibility that the clay violin (mini synthesizer) was possibly played by Vipin Reshammiya, father of Himesh Reshammiya, as he was the only one playing that instrument those days.

62

And now he had another challenge. The director had been so excited about it that he was practically jumping about like a child. He had taken great pains to explain the scene in detail.

All photographs S.M.M. Ausaja

S.D. Burman with Kishore Kumar, whose voice came to the limelight under SD's baton

Dilip Kumar, S.D. Burman and Lata Mangeshkar

S.D. Burman at a recording

S.D. Burman, Amitabh Bachchan and Hrishikesh Mukherjee: They created magic with *Abhimaan*

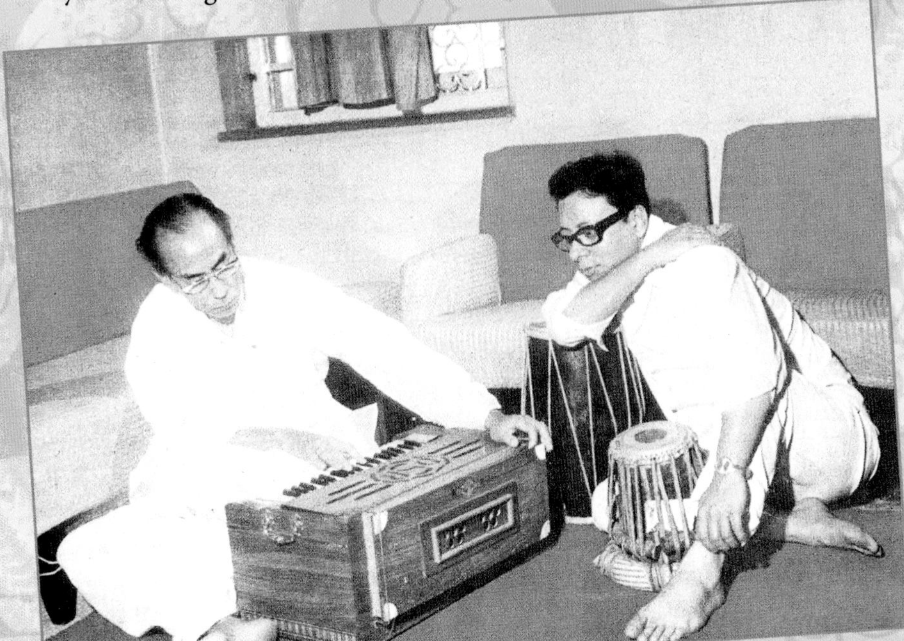

Father and son

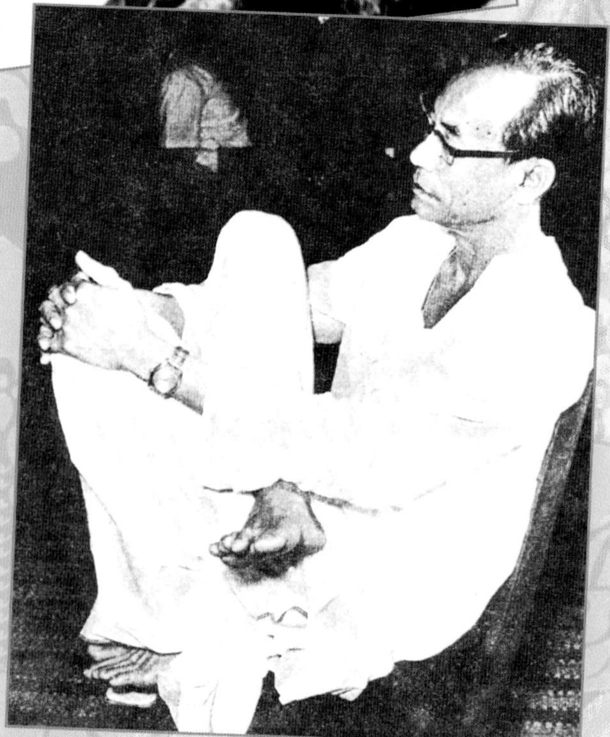

So that the songs could be crafted. There would be no scenes with dialogues to show the audience that the relationship between Rosie and Raju was strained. He had betrayed her trust; she had found out about it. She could not understand the change that had come over him, she had not known him at all. He on his part told himself he had done it in the best interest, to preserve their relationship. But as she had grown in stature from suppressed wife to dancer who had won acclaim, to a performer who could command a good fee, she had changed. The meekness had been replaced by a fierce individuality. He could not fathom her mind any more; she kept her thoughts to herself.

Goldie's idea was to express all of this through dance. Waheeda would say her bit in song, as part of her dance number; and Dev Anand would respond in song. '"I just want to continue one song after another and let the situation build up that way"–that was Goldie's idea,' Manohari Singh said in an interview, adding that even arranging and setting the two songs properly was a task that took quite some time.

It was not a duet–that was made clear. It was a back-to-back song sequence, two separate numbers, sung individually by the protagonists.

It was a challenge all right.

He mulled over it. The dance demanded a classical base. It was a plaint, so he would need a raga to match the mood. He had done it often enough before: falling back on the long tradition of raagpradhan that Bengal music composers had used since the nineteenth century.

♫

When Wajid Ali Shah, Nawab of Lucknow, was dethroned by the British in 1856 and banished to Metiabruz in Kolkata, he had spent the thirty-year exile patronizing his beloved music, specially dhrupad, khayal, tappa and thumri. Classical music found roots in the Bengal cultural soil, and influenced the music considerably, giving rise to the style where composers used a classical base to create a song for a situation, be it dance or story.

SD himself was well versed in this; had done it effectively in earlier films. '*Pavan diwani*', the opening dance number in *Dr Vidya*, or '*Mitwa*' in *Devdas*. He would use the same impetus here, combining a classical raga with a melody. But he would go one step further: take the story forward riding on its tune.

When he had finally set the music, it was a powerfully eloquent mosaic … emotion colouring the movement, as the notes flowed from a musing to a reproach. Culling a page from a past memory that held the same sentiments of unspoken reproach and distancing from someone close, he borrowed from the tune of the song he had composed in 1957, '*Pag thumak chalat balkhaye*', the same song that had caused the rift between him and his Lata. Perhaps the memory made it so easy to bring in the emotion required.

He sat at his music as always. A durrie on the floor, the harmonium on it, he in his white dhoti and kurta with folded legs, sitting bolt upright, as if for meditation. Eyes closed, mind weaving through the intricate patterns of music that resided in the whirls and whorls of his subconscious. He evoked them, asking that they nudge his creativity.

And the music flowed.

Everything that had to be said would be contained in the song, he told himself as he completed the tune, and the words, when they came would embellish the mood further, elaborating it.

He would not be disappointed. Shailendra took up where he had handed over the mood. '*Mose chhal kiye jaaye*', with the emphasis on *kiye* coming as it did perfectly suggesting anger, petulance, and disappointment all in one swift stretch of the word.

That was simple enough, he thought, after he had created Rosie's song.

But he had a repartee to follow it with. The mood would be different. He toyed with a series of ragas that could set off the Jhinjoti he had chosen for '*Mose chhal kiye jaaye*'. He hummed under his breath for days, walking up and down the rooms, his clothes swishing behind him like echoes, as he tried to find the perfect foil.

It was quite by accident he stumbled upon the solution.

Watching a window open slowly in the breeze, he caught his own image first on one side, then the other of the pane of glass.

Yes, he mused, they are saying the same thing, but saying it differently, but it is the same reflection, the same emotions are reflected in both of them.

That was it! He leapt with joy, crying out loud, startling Meera who came running. His eyes flashing, his skin shining with the discovery, he looked half fearful, but she knew him well enough not to worry.

'You got the answer?' she said, smiling. 'Of course you would.'

He hurried to the harmonium. 'Come, sit by me,' he said, 'and listen.'

She looked at him, puzzled. It was not her habit to sit beside him when he composed; her tasks lay elsewhere around the house, and even in music. But she complied. Karta was not a man to be denied, in such a mood, specially.

He played the tune. 'This is what I have composed for Rosie,' he said. And then again, 'And this is for Dev, for Raju.'

The tune in the same raga, yet...

She smiled. It would work wonderfully. Only her Karta could think this way, she thought, and let him play the tune, again and again, in its two versions, while she sat, invisible forgotten.

♫

'*Guide* is one of the finest melodious films of Hindi cinema,' says Shekhar Sen, a well-known connoisseur of cinema and music, in an interview by Moti Lalwani. 'Take the song "*Mose chhal*", which is in the typical raagpradhan genre, where Bangla songs were given a classical base. The taal and orchestration are classical and the song unfolds completely in classical mode. Yet, it shows how with a sweet melody you can still express your hatred. She was able to convince Dev Anand that she really hated him. And the reaction to that, only S.D. Burman could have done that. Just three runs of violin and the same melody from different key notes is composed for Rafi Sahib for the male song. The same tune, but no one realizes that they are listening to another song in the same tune just in a different scale, just in a male voice!

'In drama we are taught that one sentence can be rendered

in many ways. It is easily done in dialogue, in words. Doing the same thing in music is very tough. Pure music after all is a amoorat madhyam, it has no form, and cannot be expressed by the face. You can show anger on the face when delivering an angry dialogue, but a singer cannot show anger. The melody has to speak eloquently enough to portray the emotion. He did that in the song.

'Or take the song "*Tere mere sapne ab ek rang hain*". With one word, the entire song becomes a classic. The word is "hum", it plays the same role that the eyes play in a portrait–by being the centre of attraction. Eyes in most portraits have a magnetic effect, they draw you to the painting. In the song "*Tere mere sapne ab ek rang hain / ho jahan bhi le jaayen raahen hum sung hain*", the song is about the man singing to the woman, it is very private, a statement of an emotion shared between them. But a clever composer knows how to make the most of the lyrics and express much beyond what they say in the film.

'S.D. Burman knew that he was not singing the song, a singer would sing it in a film. It will be sung by the hero in a story, in a scene where there would be a different kind of lighting, and camera would capture the scene, and it would all be quite distant from him. But he thought, I will compose the song in such a manner that when the "hum" comes, every man who loves a woman will identify with it. That is why he put the emphasis on "hum", taking the tune through the one word in such a way that Rafi could put emotion in it, getting just a bit husky.

'Even the music, as Manohari-da's piece starts and Shiv Kumar joins in wonderfully with the santoor, everything is so well blended.'

63

In an interview with *Filmfare* in May 1999, Vijay Anand spoke of how when he narrated the script of *Guide* to lyricist Shailendra, whom he wished to sign on to write the songs for the film, the writer said, 'Aaj phir jeene ki tamana hai, aaj phir marne ka irada hai'. 'In those two lines he delivered for me the essence of Rosie's character,' Goldie said.

There was no doubt that Shailendra brought to the film, the characters and the music, immense depth, using his words to reveal subtle nuances. Goldie had earlier approached Hasrat Jaipuri, known for his ability to write lyrical poems on women and love, but the writer had not been able to understand the role that Waheeda was to play. Seeing her in the negative light of one who enters into an adulterous relationship, he had turned down the film, making Goldie wonder if he would indeed find a sympathetic writer.

Luckily for him, Shailendra, who was also S.D. Burman's favourite lyricist, proved to be that man. Shailendra, in the composer's own words, 'Had a unique talent and could express deep and serious expressions through very simple and easy lyrics. Common music lovers could very easily pick up and remember them ... Whatever Shailendra wrote for me was plain and simple ... even with my Hindi I could fully visualize his imagination.'

Perhaps a lesser writer would have baulked at not just the character his words would have to bring to life, but also at some of the twists and turns that the music took, as S.D. Burman, who had risen phoenix-like from a long hibernation and a life-threatening heart attack, tried experiments that would prove to the world that he was still the maestro.

Taking a calculated risk, deciding to do the never-done-before thing, the composer started the song which Rosy sings to reaffirm her decision to live, after a failed suicide attempt, with an antara. Shailendra rose to the occasion.

In a delectable blue sari and blouse ensemble that suggests youthfulness and hope, Rosy leans precariously from a haystack atop a moving vehicle; in the following stanza she walks to the edge of a wall, and is perilously close to losing her balance as she dances through the song. All this while, Raju looks on, alternately alarmed and indulgent.

Reports have it that Waheeda has a fear of heights and needed much persuasion to go through the scene, but such is the magic of the song, and the actresses' own dedication, that she practically embodied the words in her actions, both in reel and real life! It is with this scene, with S.D. Burman's heady tune combined with the line that had come spontaneously to Shailendra to encapsulate her personality, that Goldie Anand ensured that the audience, till then wary of a woman who can desert her educated husband, began to slowly fall in love with Rosie.

Perhaps, equally amazing is the fact that the song – perhaps the most popular in a film where every composition is a masterpiece – was written after the shooting had already begun. Goldie and Dev Anand had repaired to Jaipur, the composer had in his usual humility apologized for not having the song ready, but added, 'Please depend on me. I will send a tune that the world will remember.'

The Anand brothers had no option but to agree. Working the tune till he got it exactly where he wanted it, S.D. Burman recorded the song in Lata's voice and sent the spools across.

And till today, almost fifty years since he composed it, the song can be heard on any radio station, AM or FM, more often than one thinks.

In a TV interview to CNN-IBN, Waheeda remarked that the song had captured the mood perfectly: 'That song had that (expression) pinjre ki bahar chidiya nikal gayi aur jaldi se udke door chale jaana chahti hai, ki wapas pinjre mien na aa jaye. Woh bhi usmein … that feeling that was conveyed so beautifully in the words, picturization, music, the way Lata-ji sang and I think it was perfect absolutely.'

Incidentally, Waheeda has also recorded the fact that the duet '*Gaata rahe mera dil*' in *Guide* was added afterwards after all the shooting for the film was completed.

It was something that happened almost by accident.

In an interview given to Peeyush Sharma in Calcutta during the 1990s, at the venue of an international film festival, Vijay Anand revealed how this came to be: 'It had been many months since Kishore Kumar had recorded any song with either Dev Anand or S.D. Burman. There was no real cause for it; perhaps because he was very troubled by his wife Madhubala's ill health and was not able to give time for rehearsals and recordings. And Rafi had fitted in so well into *Guide* … But Dev was missing his voice, had been missing his presence and decided to meet him, and went across to his house.'

Knowing Dev Anand's ebullient love of life and infectious zest, Kishore Kumar must have been unable to resist as he was literally dragged to S.D. Burman's house.

'Dada had a very magnanimous and generous personality,' Vijay Anand said. 'The moment he saw Kishore, he said,

"Where have you been all these days?" He said this in Bangla and embraced him. They were very close, Dada and Kishore.'

True to his style, S.D. Burman then persuaded Kishore to start rehearsing, they would record a song! Right then, even as they spoke, the composer made Dev Anand and Pancham sit down and, sitting at his harmonium, started composing '*Khwaab ho tum ya koi haqeeqat, kaun ho tum batlaao*'.

'This then was the first song Kishore recorded for Dev Anand and S.D. Burman after a very long break. He sang so wonderfully, he won all our hearts,' Vijay Anand recounted. 'This was what we had been missing, both Dev Bhai and the rest of us. Burman Dada kissed his forehead; he was so happy. It was then that Dev Bhai remembered that *Guide* would release before *Teen Deviyan*, as the latter film still had some work left to be completed. Besides, *Teen Deviyan* was a smaller film, mounted on a smaller canvas, being shot in black and white; *Guide* was a much bigger film, mounted on a larger frame, in colour, and the publicity it had been getting made it a much-awaited film. Why not have a song by Kishore in *Guide* too! Then we recorded "*Gaata rahe mera dil*", shot and added the scene. The song was a huge hit.'

Perhaps as in other films, but more so in *Guide*, the fact that S.D. Burman was an integral part of the creation of the film's mood, helped mesh the songs so closely into the texture of the film.

In the same interview, Vijay Anand explained how a scene or script would be finalized only after the composer was also consulted … what the situation of the song would be, what backdrop it would be shot against, how the characters would be dressed, what the dialogues would be before and after the song, who would be in the scene, what was the purpose of the song—he would want to know everything, and everything would be first discussed with Burman Dada, before he even started composing the song.

'His input on every aspect was very important to us,' Vijay Anand said. 'Many a time, on his advice, we changed the situation of a song, or changed slightly the content of the story. His understanding of cinema, especially songs and music was very mature. He would immediately conceptualize the steps of a dance, the style, the rhythm and the execution, and then tell us about it. We respected his opinion a great deal.'

And often, too, the Anand brothers would be witness to the ceaseless fount of Dada Burman's music.

'We would sit in front of him on the floor, on a kaleen spread out for us, and he would start composing,' Vijay Anand recollected. 'And we would be in a quandary. Here we were, planning to choose five or six songs, and he had presented us with ten or twenty, each more lovely and haunting than the next. He mesmerized us with his voice and his composition.'

There is one more story about *Guide*'s songs: the first song to be composed for the film, '*Din dhal jaye*', a song to layer a poignant, eloquent scene that would be shot with restraint and finesse by the director, when the time for it came. S.D. Burman was pleased with his composition. The tune had dummy words, lines by Hafeez Jalandhari, to indicate the mood: '*Hum hi mein thi koi baat, jo yaad na tum ko aa sake / tum ne hum ko bhula diya, hume tumhe bhula sake.*'

But this time his director and producer were not quite as happy with what he played to them. Perhaps, the tune did not convey the subtle pathos that Goldie wanted for the scene. I like it, Dada Burman said, and left.

But the thought rankled, his song had not been accepted hundred per cent.

Humbling himself, the composer called Dev Anand from his house. Maybe they had a point, he would try another tune.

Working through the night, he composed a substitute and went back with it next day. A harmonium was arranged, and S.D. Burman, settling in front of it, played his new tune. The brothers liked it. Shailendra was called, sent off with the tune and came back in five minutes with the complete lyrics! The first song for the film was ready!

Despite the passion they put into *Guide*, the film stumbled in the first few days of its release, though it released to full houses, thanks to all the excitement the pre-release publicity for the film had whipped up. The audience could not quite understand much of what was being presented to them; a woman who leaves her husband for a guide, a protagonist who is jailed for forgery and who dies just when he has done something that makes you like him. Vijay Anand went on record saying that it was one of the worst moments of his life: the deafening silence that marked the hall as the audience left it, at the film's ending. Mostly, it was the ending. Dev Anand was a happy-go-lucky hero, playing lighter roles till then, he was not Dilip Kumar, dying miserable and pitifully at the end of many of his tragic films. But as the days passed into weeks, the film gathered strength; audiences, especially in the metros, began to realize that here was a film story with a difference. The magic of the acting, the songs took hold. Before long, *Guide* was well on its way to becoming a success at the box office.

At the Filmfare Awards, the film reaped seven trophies. Even the unconventional character of Rosie seemed to find acceptance, culminating in an award for Waheeda.

B.K. Karanjia, when he called Waheeda to tell her she had won the award over Suchitra Sen, nominated for her double role in *Mamta*, added that while Suchitra Sen's two roles were sympathetic, Waheeda had essayed a role that 'by Indian standards was not a very sympathetic role. But you left a mark, the character is so beautiful, you don't feel or you don't hate that character. So, that is the challenge.'

But there was still disappointment in store.

Incredibly, the music lost out. And that too to a musical score as nondescript as *Suraj*, remembered today for just one Rafi number, '*Baharon phool barsaon*'. One would be hard-pressed to recall another song from the film. In contrast, all the numbers of *Guide* continue to be hummed even now. For the second time in his career, with a score that could not be faulted on any count, S.D. Burman lost to another music director.

So keen was the disappointment of the *Guide* team over the fact that Dada Burman was not given the award for his music that the entire team was in shock. Those days the awards were disclosed earlier, not at the function itself. Nargis had already phoned Dada up, telling him he was getting the award. Then the awards were made public. *Guide* had won seven awards, but Dada's name was not among the seven.

What had happened? What could have happened?

Waheeda said in an interview, 'I phoned Dev, Dev called me, Vijay Anand called me, the lines were busy with our phone calls back and forth. It was unthinkable, Dada's music should have got the award, every song was brilliant, there was not one that could be said was better than the other, you could not compare one song with the other to judge which was better; the music as a whole sparkled. We decided to boycott the Filmfare Award function. We would not go, in protest. Then I don't know who, Karanjia or Jain, whoever was the *Filmfare* editor then spoke to Dev. I think that must be the reason, Dev called and said, "No, Waheeda, it is too late now to do anything like this, there will be too much gadbad, we are getting awards in seven departments, we must go." We were, however, very upset, seven departments of the film yes, but the one who should definitely have got it, was left out.'

Waheeda says she met Dada after the ceremony and expressed her disappointment over his being missed out.

'He was composed, and his face was genuinely calm. He said it mattered little. I told him we had planned to miss the function, to boycott it. He said, "Yes, I know, Dev has told me about it, Goldie too, what you had planned together; and it was very sweet of you, but it makes no difference to me, I don't care. And these things happen all the time. It makes no difference because I know and the whole world knows that my songs are very good!"'

64

Pandit Shiv Kumar Sharma shares an observation in an interview with Moti Lalwani and Richa Lakhanpal:

This is something I heard. That when Dada was given the Filmfare Award (perhaps in 1973 for *Abhimaan*), music director

Shankar rang up to congratulate him, 'Dada, congratulations for the Filmfare Award,' to which Dada replied, 'Shankar, thank you. But there is one thing I will tell you, I did not spend any money. I got it genuinely.'

Maybe it was in his mind that Shankar-Jaikishan must have done something, bought a huge number of copies of *Filmfare* to fill in the votes, or something like that, as they had won in the previous years rather frequently.

There was an interview on the Internet with Pyarelal in which he admits that Lakshmi-ji had told him to buy copies of *Filmfare* and fill the forms, nominating themselves. He said, 'It made kachra of us, devalued our worth and integrity a lot, but after the award, we got a lot of work.'

Besides, when *Suraj* and *Guide* were nominated the same year for best music, Dada was also approached by a young fellow, 'Ki aapko award mil sakta hai, magar kharcha karna padega.' Dada replied, 'Young man, I want this award, but I will not buy it! I can spend that money in a better way!'

Which is why when Shankar congratulated him, Dada said, 'Shankar, Thank you, but I did not spend any money!'

Incidentally, Shankar-Jaikishan would be at it again in the Filmfare Awards for 1972, when they got their film *Be-imaan* the award for best music, in a year that had *Pakeezah* as a contender!

65

If I was a child, I would have been sent to bed, I think. All is quiet at home. The instruments are silent; there is no sound from the kitchen either. No hiss of frying, no clatter of pans.

Even the fan that goes krr-krr overhead seems to be whispering today.

I am also silent. But it is because I want to let my mind think. Was I wrong in what I did?

Let me rewind the spool a bit.

It is ten o' clock in the morning. Most of the musicians are present, with two latecomers hurrying in, hands folded in apology. I am tolerant; it's not easy being punctual in this city. Anything can delay a person. I understand that. As long as intentions are good and effort is made, it is fine by me.

Everything is set. But where is Pancham? He cannot be late in his own house!

The father in me is worried for him. He is talented, amazingly talented, in music. I think he has talent from both of us, his parents, in good measure. How can I forget the time when as a chubby boy of eleven he told me he could play the mouth organ. And he dared to play it on my telling him to, no fear stopped his breath short. Such confidence.

He has proved his love for music. He trained, as I told him to, in the tabla, in the santoor, in all aspects of the classical.

He has imbibed music from the very first breath he took, and since he came to live with his mother and me, has been steeped in music.

How I train him is something he does not realize. I make him assist me, make him sit by me while I compose, make him listen at rehearsals, to work in the recording, in the arranging of music for recording. It is a part of his training. I know it will come to good use when he starts to fly.

But where will my Pancham fly? Two films after *Chhote Nawab*, he is still waiting to take to the skies. Meanwhile, I continue his training.

Does he realize that? I wonder.

'Is it frustration that makes him behave the way he does?' Meera asked me last week as we waited in bed, unable to sleep, because our son had not yet come home. She got up to go to the window so many times, but came back with a sigh, and then asked me the question.

I had no answer. No response or reason to give for Pancham going to discos and noisy places every evening. What could he hope to find there? The company of his peers? The sounds there are so loud, so alien to his upbringing. Is there a rebel then in this son of mine? As I had always suspected?

Of course, he would be late. I do not know what time he comes back, but it is too late for him to be up and still manage to get to the studio in time. It has happened before.

Today, I paced the room, my usual calm rippled as if a stone had fallen into it. The stone of worry weighed with impatience. I do not like to keep my musicians waiting.

When he did arrive and we started work, he was not concentrating.

I think my calm broke at that point. I did not shout. I don't think I have ever shouted in my life at anyone. But I was sharp. Cutting in my words. I saw Pancham look at me, his round eyes looking rounder. His face flushed, and he threw a quick look at the musicians. They were all pretending they had not heard.

I tried telling Meera that in the studio Pancham is not a son; he is an assistant. And I require complete dedication. But a mother's heart…

So, now there is silence.

My son, my son, how can I help you!

Have I been a bad father, I wonder … too lost in my own work, my world of music. Have I failed you in any way?

I do not think I have. But I am afraid.

What if you never get your chance to fly?

66

The story of how he rebuked his son and assistant, R.D. Burman, for engaging twelve musicians instead of the eleven he had specified, and how he insisted on going ahead with only eleven, after paying off the twelfth and sending him back, is rather well known. S.D. Burman always gave simplicity in rendition great value, be it in the interpretation and unfolding of the music or the singer's rendition.

In Majrooh's words, from an interview by Peeyush Sharma, courtesy Moti Lalwani: 'Dada did not like too many instruments, he would try and use as few as possible. At some point, Pancham took on the responsibility of arranging for the orchestration, but often Dada would remove some of the musicians, saying, "If you load a song with so much jewellery, you won't see the song at all. Take it away." He would say, lessen a violin here, cut the percussion, things like that.'

Obviously, the director had to say this often enough. Pandit Shiv Kumar Sharma adds that SD often compared the orchestration to the bindi on a beautiful woman's face. She may be beautiful and dressed in lovely clothes, but if the bindi she wears is too big it will hide the beauty of her face, he would explain.

Yet, in his next film, *Jewel Thief*, he would do what he had done with the snake dance in *Guide*: use an entire orchestra to create a mood that was both eloquent and musical.

The composer was riding the crest of a wave again. His creativity was at a new high, the songs of *Guide* resounded from radios many times a day, and his next film for Dev Anand, *Teen Deviyan*, too was making waves. Though the film had three heroines and one hero who was quite a match for them all, it did not create any box office history; however, its music, alternating between the emotions of romantic love, hesitation, playful teasing and flirtation, proved winsome enough to stay in public memory. Dada Burman used Rafi as well as Kishore Kumar in the film, with Asha Bhonsle as the perfect foil in the duets. The range SD traversed, from the playful Kishore ditty '*Khwab ho tum ya*', to the pensive Rafi solo '*Kahin bekhayal hokar*', from Kishore's drenched in mischief '*Arre yaar meri*' to the utterly romantic Rafi number '*Aise toh na dekho*', and won for him yet another BFJA Award.

But it was with *Jewel Thief* that Dada Burman would make history again.

Jewel Thief had two heroines. Vijay Anand had cast the ebullient Tanuja as a foil to the more layered role for Vyjayanthimala, who would play the main lead opposite Dev Anand. Dev himself had Ashok Kumar's weighty screen presence to offset his mischievous and mysterious role as the suspected jewel thief.

An engaging, fast-paced thriller, *Jewel Thief* was completely the kind of film that would bring out the best in director Vijay Anand, the theme giving enough scope for music of every mood.

And S.D. Burman was ready for the challenge.

If the song *'Yeh dil na hota bechara'* came out of a viewing of David Lean's *Bridge on the River Kwai* which he watched with his son, *'Raat akeli hai'* emerged from a childhood memory, as did so many of S.D. Burman's songs.

The story goes about *'Yeh dil na hota bechara'* that on their way back after watching the film, the irrepressible Pancham kept drumming on the car's dashboard and whistling his own versions of the signature marching tune from the film which in turn set off his father's imagination, resulting in the song that Dev Anand sings as he walks on the road, blocking the way for an irate Tanuja's car! Though the song is a perfect fit in its present setting in *Jewel Thief*, it was not really composed with Dev Anand in mind. More likely, if things had gone differently, Guru Dutt would have been the star on whom it would have been shot.

S.D. Burman had indeed composed the song for GD Films' *Baharen Phir Bhi Ayengi*, but both the composer and the song had been abandoned when the composer had his heart attack. Anxious to keep his film rolling, Guru Dutt signed on O.P. Nayyar, who had scored for *Mr and Mrs 55* earlier.

When he found the situation working well for the song, the composer grafted it onto *Jewel Thief*.

Taking the personalities of the heroines as clear opposites, the composer decided to give them songs that would add brush strokes to the characterization.

Vyjayanthimala, confused, nursing a secret grief and an obvious love for the hero, would sing softer numbers like *'Rulake gaya sapna mera'*, and *'Dil pukare'*, the duet with Rafi. At the climax of the film, emboldened by the need to seek out her captive brother, she dances with a frenzy close to abandon, yet there is a classic majesty in her movements. The scene suited S.D. Burman completely. It gave him a chance to fall back on the rustic music he so loved, and use instruments that would recall the flavour of the regions of the eastern Himalayas.

Using a pantheon of percussion instruments like the Bangla dhol, Burmese dhol, tabla tarang, he created a dance number that had the climax almost built into its rhythm. Touches of Tibetan music were added and the Nepali drum procured for the right sound that he wanted to create. Such was his command on the medium and on the minds of his director and producer: what Dada Burman wanted for his song, Dada Burman got!

Manohari Singh recalled in an interview with Moti Lalwani and Richa Lakhanpal, also reproduced in H.Q. Chowdhury's book, *Incomparable Sachin Dev Burman*: 'Easily he used 60-70 musicians, it was amazing. He was his own example.' When S.D. Burman wanted to bend his rules, he did it in full measure, and created magic in the process.

But it was the song that the maestro composed for Tanuja that proved his mettle as a composer who could compete with those half his age.

Vijay Anand's prescription was for a song with a difference. And S.D. Burman decided to deliver just the right mixture!

Picture the scene: Tanuja, the boss's daughter, has a crush on the young handsome man who is charming but seems not quite interested. Being a confident, spoilt brat, who cannot take no for an answer, she decides on an impromptu seduction. Which man, she thinks, can resist her combination of looks, sex appeal and money!

The song, *'Raat akeli hain'*, could have easily been one of the crooning numbers Asha Bhonsle had quite made her trademark. Great songs sung extremely seductively, but there would be no element of surprise. Also the roles played by the crooners were mainly either vamps or women with negative shades to their personality. Tanuja was different, her role was quite a breakaway from the other supporting roles in most films; the song demanded something sensational.

The childlike quality in Tanuja possibly inspired the composer to delve into childhood games, and come up with the form his song would take. Children in that era often played a game in which they would whisper in someone's ear, and suddenly yell to startle them. Tanuja's song would borrow from that innocent prank.

Asha Bhonsle's rendition of the low whisper, spoken rather than sung, as a start to a song that would get feet tapping with its beat, is incomparable, even when placed against her own vast repertoire. The whisper, seductive and secretive, bursts into a crescendo, and even a resisting Dev Anand is forced to watch momentarily the shimmering, gyrating girl–woman vying for his attention.

And perhaps the most enduring accompaniment to the song came from the skilful blending of the saxophone, played by his assistant and ace instrumentalist Manohari Singh. How often does someone humming this song (a difficult number but so irresistible) find that the humming includes the saxophone interludes too! That's how well the instrument was blended into the composition.

With this song, S.D. Burman proved that Western or tribal, rural or classical, when it came to music, he was lord of them all!

67

Scenes from music sittings, based on an interview of music director Sapan Sengupta (of the 1970s' composer duo Sapan–Jagmohan) by Moti Lalwani and Richa Lakhanpal.

Location: The Burman home, living room.

Characters: S.D. Burman, in characteristic white dhoti kurta, on a durrie spread on the floor. Beside him, Pancham on the tabla, on the same durrie. On another durrie on the other side, his assistant Suhrid is on the harmonium.

S.D. Burman is singing, he tries out a tune, then stops to embellish it. The harmonium plays along. Pancham waits, hands on the ready, eyes on his father, for a nod to begin playing.

Suddenly, S.D. Burman stops. His eyes open, he turns his head a little and looks at Suhrid.

S.D. Burman: You are sitting with the harmonium, playing, Suhrid, where is your ma?

Suhrid *(puzzled for a moment)*: My mother is in Calcutta.

S.D. Burman: Hutt, I am asking about the 'ma' in the harmonium. Have you forgotten it in the composition? Where is the madhyam in the instrument?

Confused and worried, Suhrid looks at his fingers on the harmonium.

S.D. Burman: Where is your ma, Suhrid. Where is it going? Is it teevre or shudh, where has the ma gone?

Suhrid lifts his eyes to the composer, and touches his ear with his hand to denote he is sorry.

S.D. Burman smiles and Suhrid returns to the tune he was playing.

♫

Another scene, based on an interview of Pandit Hari Prasad Chaurasia by Moti Lalwani and Richa Lakhanpal.

SCENE I

Again set in same living room. This time, S.D. Burman is in a dhoti and ganji (vest), sitting alone on his durrie; a phalanx of musicians arranged on another durrie. A rehearsal session is on, music colours the entire room, permeating every corner. From beyond, the sound of cooking can be heard, the hiss of vegetables being put into hot oil, the soft clink of a spoon, the clatter of a vessel being put down hastily…

The door opens, and a man appears. He enters softly, a bit bent in his effort to be invisible.

Burman notices the change in the air, though his eyes are closed. He looks up to see the visitor.

S.D. Burman: Aree, Hari, aao, baitho.

Hariprasad Chaurasia sits down.

S.D. Burman: Have you eaten anything?

Hari Prasad: Burman-da, I have not yet eaten. I will go home and eat. I am coming straight from work at All India Radio.

S.D. Burman: No, no *(turns to call over his shoulder)*. Meera, get a plate quickly.

Meera comes out carrying a dinner plate. Burman picks up a tin of rasagollas that have obviously come for him from Calcutta and empties the entire tin onto the plate, placing each sweet one by one carefully, to get the maximum advantage of the space on the plate.

The musicians who have been playing turn their eyes towards the appetizing sweets.

S.D. Burman: Arey, Hari, take some, help yourself.

Hariprasad *(looks around at the musicians and realizes they are too respectful of the composer to reach for the tempting sweets)*: No, Dada, it is okay, let it be.

S.D. Burman goes back to the rehearsing. The music starts again.

S.D. Burman: Hari, eat, take it. Or flies will sit on it.

Hariprasad then gingerly picks up a rasogulla and signals the other musicians to help themselves too. The musicians respond that they are fine, not hungry.

Hariprasad: Okay, you all are not hungry, but I am. I have come straight from All India Radio, and not had lunch. And these are from Calcutta, so soft and yielding, melting in the mouth. I cannot resist them.

He reaches out and takes one more, then one more, and yet another. Meanwhile, the rehearsal resumes and the music flows on. Before anyone realizes, the plate is empty. The music pauses.

S.D. Burman: Shall I call for anything else?

Hariprasad: No, no, I am done.

SCENE II

The next day. Recording room. Everything is being set for recording.

Lata Mangeshkar sits beside S.D. Burman, who is singing and teaching her the new song that is to be recorded. They sing alternately for some time. Almost done, Lata Mangeshkar gets up to prepare herself for the recording.

Then the composer pauses, and looks up.

S.D. Burman: Hari, O Hari, come here. Listen to this song, you have to play the flute for it.

Hariprasad draws close and sits down.

S.D. Burman: Lata, come here. Listen to him, he plays very sweetly. How sweetly he is playing…

Lata Mangeshkar: Yes, Dada, I know.

S.D. Burman: Yesterday, he was at my house and ate so many sweets, little wonder he is playing so sweetly.

Lata Mangeshkar: What is this, Hari, what is Dada saying?

Hari Prasad: I ate up all his favourite rasagollas yesterday. I was so hungry. I thought he did not mind. But he is taking his revenge now!

Lata Mangeshkar *(laughing)*: It is his little joke, Hari. You should not mind it!

68

Suddenly, he was wide awake. Something in him was uneasy. His brow knitted, he prepared to go on his regular morning walk. He had planned to drop in on Shivkumar Sharma later. But he was disturbed. And could not put his finger on it.

He was driving to Sharma's house when it came to him. The dream. Something he had dreamt had been so disturbing. His body jolted back, grappling with the memory of it, his hands were shaking.

He drew the car to a halt on the side of the road. Under the shade of a spreading gulmohar, he sat in his car. A bird flew overhead, startled by the sound of his car engine. And he remembered! His head spun a little with the violence of the memory.

Then, it came to him vividly ... the recording room, the music, a song he could not now recollect, a hauntingly beautiful tune, he could hear the violin on a high note, drawing itself out.

And he had turned to smile at Pancham, through the glass, and suddenly the boy was not there.

The music had stopped; he had lifted a hand and stilled it in mid note. The musicians had silenced themselves at once. He remembered the half-raised violin bow, the still blown cheeks of the saxophone player, the half-lifted flute poised in the air, frozen at his command. His eyes had darted about, was the boy playing a prank...

And a bird had hopped out from behind the sound control system, and looked him in the eye. With round eyes ... round, round, like Pancham's.

He felt a cry rising in his throat, but the bird had taken one little hop, turned away, and making a quick semicircle had flown out, out, out through the closed soundproof door…

'Flown' … he whispered.

What could it mean? His brow felt damp, he wiped it. I must be getting sick, he thought, or old.

It was only a dream.

Turning the key, he started the Fiat, and drove on.

All day, the unease sat by his side, looking at him like a bird with round eyes.

When the crow that always came to ask for food at the kitchen window cawed that afternoon, he got up and walking across chased it away. Then, he shut the window.

69

'Let us go to the old man, who can be managed within our means,' Shakti Samanta has quoted while recounting the reason why instead of Shankar-Jaikishan he approached S.D. Burman for his next venture. It was to be a quickie, a jhatphat film on which the producer did not want to spend too much.

There is a well-known story about how S.D. Burman told Shakti Samanta that he had raised his price, and asked if the producer could quite afford him now. It must have pulled the rug from under Samanta's feet, that statement, but he waited to know more. 'He was a man who never hiked up his price,' Samanta said, recalling the episode. 'One day when I went to sign him for my next film, he said, "I have hiked up my price. I cannot work for you at the amount you were paying me." He lectured me for about fifteen minutes, then I asked him how much he would charge me. He asked me for Rs 5,000 more. I was amazed; it was such a small amount. He looked at me and said, "Is that too much? Okay, pay me what you paid me earlier." He was such a lovable man and so innocent.'

Shakti Samanta must have heaved a huge sigh of relief; he had kept aside a lakh for the music.

A lakh! The composer was delighted and told Samanta, 'In that case you will get music that will be remembered forever!'

The film of course would go down in the history of cinema for a number of reasons.

In a more recent interview, a repeat broadcast of Vividh Bharati's programme *Aaj Ke Fankar*, broadcast on 13 January 2011, the producer quoted one more reason why he decided in favour of S.D. Burman rather than his other composers.

'The subject was such and it was a Bengali story. Sachin Karta had done super job in both Dev Anand films *Guide* and *Jewel Thief* and I really wanted to go back to him. Also, Nayyar was never a choice for a Bengali subject, neither were Shankar-Jaikishan. In *Aradhana*, Sachin Karta gave me my life's biggest hit. I made so much money that I produced my next five films only from the music sale of *Aradhana*. Of course, the film was a huge hit also. You know, the record was dubbed and released in five languages, and was a hit in every language.'

Aradhana, the 'quickie', was to make the career of its hero Rajesh Khanna, setting him off on a trajectory that would see him shining as a superstar through the next decade. It also gave Kishore Kumar a huge boost, lifting him firmly to the status of the voice of the era; in coming years, Kishore Kumar would sing for Rajesh Khanna through all his hits, and become the voice of every star including the phenomenon called Amitabh Bachchan.

In an interview to *Screen* on the eleventh anniversary of Kishore Kumar's death, Rajesh Khanna spoke with unrestrained fondness of the manner in which Kishore so beautifully reflected his persona's character. 'When I heard the first song of *Aradhana*, I felt as though I was actually singing. Or that he's standing in front of me and I'm copying him. We were like two lives in one body.'

S.D. Burman used Kishore Kumar in *Aradhana* as his 'second serve'. He was of course still very fond of tennis, which he had given up so long ago.

'Tennis is one game that requires you to be extra alert,' he is quoted as saying in 'The Final Touch Made All the Difference' by Raju Bharatan, *Filmfare*, November 1975. 'It helped keep my reflexes sharp. It taught me that in music as in tennis, there are two "serves". If the first serve fails, in the second you do not try something so flashy. Sometimes my first serve clicked as in "*Hum bekhudi mein*" and "*Kya se kya ho gaya*". At other times, the second serve came into play. In *Aradhana*, I tried both serves–Rafi and Kishore. This time the second serve clicked. I had always had Kishore in reserve. Now he became my main singer.'

Another star who found his shine with the film was Anand Bakshi, till then known for the lyrics he had penned for films like *Jab Jab Phool Khile* and *Milan*, but yet far away from being considered one among those in the forefront of lyric writers. After writing for S.D. Burman's tunes in *Aradhana*, it was as if Anand Bakshi had been blessed with the composer's magic touch. He would never look back.

As for S.D. Burman, he made history too–the songs of *Aradhana*, over forty years since they were composed and played on screen for the first time, still resound in the air and the minds of music lovers.

Much has been written and said, discussed and reiterated on the songs of *Aradhana*. Were they plagiarized from Western numbers? Were they the work of Pancham passed off as that of the father?

Two of S.D. Burman's instrumentalists and arrangers, Kersi Lord, who played the piano accordion for '*Roop tera mastana*', and Manohari Singh are on record to say that not only did the senior composer create the tunes, but more likely too that even at the recording of '*Roop tera mastana*', the song that is often credited to his son, Pancham was possibly not really even present.

Kersi Lord says, 'I don't think RD was present, I don't remember seeing RD anywhere in the studios. But people say that he was there and "*Roop tera mastana*" is his song, but I don't know. Even for the song recording, he was not there.'

Kersi Lord, who was SD's assistant for the film's songs and the entire music arrangement, also said, 'No, I don't think Pancham was involved. Maybe, he might have been sitting there, I don't know, I'm not sure (about his sitting there). Everybody asks us whether RD was there, but I said, for the recording he was not there. And sitting I don't know. I didn't play only for Mr Burman. I played for all the top music directors. So, we couldn't be involved in every recording.'

Kersi Lord went on to add, 'Another thing, though I am going little bit off-track now. Somebody wrote one book in Pune, years back, on Pancham. Whatever the mistakes in that book, mistakes are there, hundred per cent, I vouch for it, those mistakes still continue. Because when anybody writes a new book, he refers to that book, so the publishing of wrong information continues.'

In a detailed interaction on the song with Moti Lalwani and Richa Lakhanpal, Manohari Singh goes on to say how a song can change from conception to final form, with the addition of the words, the inflections of the singer, the adding of rhythm…

'The shape of a song can change by the time it comes to finishing stage,' Singh said. 'Words come in with their own weightages, and as the adjustments for the words are made, a song which started in one type of tune could with all embellishments change in shape, sometimes considerably. "*Roop tera mastana*" was very much Dada's song, he composed it. Then Kishore-da offered his inputs, some weightages through emphasis, as he played around with the words, and then Dada said, "Arre Kishore, you have made it so good, you have made the tune so good."

'Kishore-da was also a great composer, a great actor, no doubt about that. He played around with the words, added emphasis or weight here or there and brought the song to a metre. The sur was not there though, so after adjustments and slowly working on it, the sur was improved and the song was made sureela again.

'This was all normal. It was always the job of assistants to suggest improvements. Whether SD approved of them or not was another matter altogether. If it was a good suggestion, he would take it. He has even added a line to accommodate a suggestion he liked. I have seen him from 1958 when I worked with him in *Sitaron Se Aage*, through *Kala Pani*, *Kala Bazaar*, and he had the same style of composing and follow-up till recording.

'The credit goes to Burman, Kersi is correct, *Aradhana*'s music was all S.D. Burman Saab's. RD was not involved in it at all. I was the assistant director for *Aradhana*. The music arrangement for the entire film was on me. Basu Chakraborty was my partner, we were known as Basu-Manohari. We created the music for films like *Sabse Bada Rupaiya* and some others.

'But (coming back to "*Roop tera mastana*"), Burman saab would leave some of the work of shaping the song to us. "This is the song, give it this shape, this form … it's a bit modern, make it a bit sexy," Burman saab would say things like this.

'So we thought, fine, and fixed the rhythm pattern. By we I mean Basu, Maruti, Pancham. Pancham was also an assistant. We all sat together and fixed the rhythm pattern then fitted it over the tune. We worked together on it. Everyone, myself, Basu, RD, Maruti contributed to this. Maruti used to look after the complete rhythm section.

'It was a great team, and assistant or arranger, all of us tried our best to our individual capacities to make a song more beautiful, that was our responsibility and we did it. My responsibility was arranging the song. To write the notation, take it forward and backward, make the score, that was my contribution. This is the main work of most assistants. Assistants have a lot to do, they contribute a lot. Whether it is for S.D. Burman or RD, we did the same, and contributed whatever we could.'

And in the composer's own words, in Sankarlal Bhattacharjee's 'A Case for Folk Music', *Hindustan Standard*,

1972: 'You have heard my famous song in *Aradhana*, "*Safal hogi teri aradhana, kahe ko roye*". It is composed on a simply Baul melody. Then there is the famous *Guide* song, "*Wahan kaun hai tera musafir jayega kahan*". That too is done on Bhatiali lines. What's more surprising is that the rather jazzy sort of hit song "*Roop tera mastana*" sung by Kishore Kumar is but a beautiful folk melody that I happened to have heard a long time ago. I remembered the tune because of its peculiar effect. It merely uses two notes and has a very special influence on the senses.'

S.D. Burman has also gone on record saying, as reported by Pulak Bandyopadhyay, 'Tell those who say I have copied "*Mere sapnon ki rani*" from "*Tequila*", that I have indeed based it on another tune, but not copied it. And it is not "*Tequila*". The tune is inspired by a song sung during a boat race in Comilla. I am a Bengali. There is a lot of musical wealth scattered all over my Bengal. I will first of all take all those before turning to the West.'

Incidentally, the episode with the extra musicians happened during one of the recordings for *Aradhana*, which adds credence to the belief that Pancham was present at least at some of the recordings to assist his father. And there is some evidence that he influenced the song's mood by adding the erotic twist into it, transforming a folk ditty sung by a young girl into a seduction sequence that could scorch the screen when played against the visuals. There are, however, enough people in both SD's and RD's teams who dispute this, making for a situation with little clarity. Manohari Singh, for example, is emphatic in an interview to Moti Lalwani and Richa Lakhanpal: 'The credit goes to Burman saab. Kersi is right. *Aradhana*'s music is entirely the work of S.D. Burman. RD was not involved at all. Kishore did give his ideas on "*Roop tera mastana*", changing the tune a bit and S.D. Burman agreed that it worked.'

Despite *Aradhana*'s musical success, the Filmfare Award continued to elude him, and unfairly so. Again, inexplicably, it was *Jeene Ki Raah* that won the year *Aradhana* was in the race!

70

He was singing again. The voice, so long kept shut except at home, suddenly found expression, released like a bird from a cage. His voice … he listened to it. The notes were like liquid, flowing into each other seamlessly, the timbre strong and clear. Not a quiver, nothing to show that at one time not so many years ago, he had felt there was not enough breath in his body to keep him alive, let alone sing.

He had a collection to sing now, a quiver full of songs to release into the world of his music lovers, and he knew each would find its mark in their hearts.

The theme song of *Aradhana* had wrought the magic, given him back his confidence, though he had realized even with *Guide* that he was in good form again. '*Safal hogi teri aradhana*' he had sung, and the words had come true once more. His film had done well, the songs were hits. His own song, in fact, had effected the change in the film's name: earlier Samanta had titled it *Subah Pyar Ki*.

And now he was recording so many more. '*Meri duniya hai maa*' for *Talash*, the film he would complete soon, and he had planned '*Prem ke pujari hum hain*' for Dev's *Prem Pujari*.

Besides, he was working once more in tandem with Meera, who was writing songs at some inspired pace. Other lyricists approached him once they knew he was recording Bangla numbers, but he realized he had to do justice to his wife's creative output first. And she was in prolific mode!

Two Bengali records for Meera's lyrics, the tunes ranging from folk songs to modern compositions with a folk base, followed. He experimented freely with the songs, they were not for any film, they were his very own, for a listener base that he had honed his talents on: the Calcutta listener. In one song he blended the mukhda into the antra, as if it was a long, long poem spoken in one breath. The following year, in 1970, the fount would continue to flow and Meera would write more songs that her husband would bedeck with his tunes and express in his inimitable style.

In the Bengali songs he found new expression for his new work in Hindi.

'*Khayi hai re humne kasam*' in *Talash* and '*Phoolon ke rang se*' in *Prem Pujari*, would flower from the Bengali originals.

71

Perhaps it is not fancy to say that S.D. Burman introduced the trend of an offbeat voice singing the occasional song, along with the accepted voices for heroes and heroines, in a film. The composer often kept as his own the songs that were not lip-synced on screen. These had a specific role in taking the story forward. The lyrics could highlight the philosophical significance of a scene or reflect the mood and thoughts of one of the protagonists. True that his style, his very enunciation and the quality of his voice was a world apart from what listeners imagined the main players in their films to sing in. But thanks to his command on his voice, his amazing ability to bring in nuances of feeling into the words and to embellish the tunes with touches that were unique, S.D. Burman's songs as commentary proved not just acceptable but popular. Through the years, from *Sujata* where he sang the beautiful love poem, '*Sun mere bandhu re*', to *Bandini* where he sang the climatic '*More saajan hain us paar*', to *Guide*'s '*Wahan kaun hai tera*', and all the way down to *Prem Pujari* and *Talash*, his voice held its haunting quality, echoing in the mind long after he had stopped singing. The slap of the oar against water, the gliding prow, the moon reflecting on the waves: his voice evoked these images even when the boatman was not his theme.

In fact so complex was his mastery over his voice and his compositions that most singers never really could match it. Kishore Kumar would often hesitate, and when asked if he was finding it difficult, would nod, and agree to the suggestion that the tune be made simpler. The composer knew the limits of each of his singers, and though he often pushed them to give their best, he also realized when to pull back and ease things, and he knew that for all his considerable talent and range of voice, Kishore was untrained.

According to Vijay Anand, in an interview by Peeyush Sharma, courtesy Moti Lalwani:

> He had a magical voice, it would be so magical an effect that we would listen endlessly, sitting with him. Lyrics for the songs would not be ready yet, but he would fill in with Bangla words and create the tunes. And mark my words, there was no singer who could

> quite match him in the entire industry. He would come up with such flourishes, such sudden nuances, it was mind blowing. When he would then sing the same tune for Lata or Rafi or Asha, he would simplify it considerably.
>
> In fact, both Lata and Kishore openly used to say to him, we just cannot sing to match you, please simplify it a bit. But Burman Dada would also insist, he would say, you can surely sing this, come and rehearse it with me.
>
> Often, Lata and Kishore would first listen to him singing before they started rehearsing. For a long time everyone would be lost in listening to the mastery of his singing. He would work really hard then, to rehearse his singers. Till he extracted the right effect, the right quality from them, he would not start recording the song. That is why his songs are eternal, and still so popular.

Taking a cue from his father's use of his voice in film songs, R.D. Burman would lend his voice to songs of quite a different tempo and mood, but again the voice would be a far cry from the genteel tones of the main singers in the films he composed for. It was a signature style that, in the late twentieth century, singer composer A.R. Rahman would adopt and personalize too, with the same effectiveness.

72

Just a sweet story

(courtesy Moti Lalwani and Richa Lakhanpal)

S.D. Burman would visit his beloved Calcutta every month, sometimes even twice a month.

Careful as he was about his possessions and belongings, he would visit his friend Sapan Sengupta to entrust him with an important assignment.

Sapan used to live on 14th Road, just behind S.D. Burman's house. He walked across often enough to look at the composer's bungalow but did not think it right to approach or disturb him, though he admired him a lot.

There was a restaurant at the corner of the road called Fairdeal. Opposite it lived writer Mukul Dutt, who also wrote *Aan Milo Sajna* starring Asha Parekh and Rajesh Khanna.

Mukul Dutt and Sapan used to sit at Fairdeal, and one day, perhaps knowing that Sapan was a great fan of S.D. Burman, Mukul Dutt took him to the composer's house to meet the maestro.

It was the beginning of a long association as, Sapan says, the composer grew very fond of him and treated him as his own son. Perhaps that is why Sapan was chosen for the unusual task that the composer wanted done.

S.D. Burman would hand over a bunch of postcards to Sapan before he embarked on his trip. There would be as many postcards as the number of days he would be away. Each postcard would have two or three lines written on them in S.D. Burman's own hand, and his Calcutta address too already put in. The lines would say: all is fine in the house, or all is well at home, or everything is all right with the house, lines to that effect.

The idea was if the missive was not posted every day and did not reach him for a day or more, something had gone amiss at his house.

'What he desired was someone responsible should go across to his bungalow and check that all was fine there. As Meera

Devi was also accompanying him, there was no other way he could keep a check on his home. So I would visit the house every single day of his being away. Then come back and post the card for that day.

'When I would go across, I would press the bell, and someone would come out to the balcony upstairs, look down and ask who has come. If it was me or someone else well known to S.D. Burman saab, they would open the door, otherwise the door would stay shut. It was a surefire way of his ensuring his peace of mind and not worrying about his house while he was in Calcutta!'

73

Tere nainaa talaash kare jise
Woh hai tujhi mein kahin deewaane

I will not compromise. I know my singers and my songs, and I know how they will work on screen. By now any director or producer who has seen my work should know that. Yet he wants me to change my mind!

Any director or producer who knows me should also know I never change my mind once it is made up, because I decide after careful deliberation. I have sometimes spent days over the decision, tried one voice, then another, and then decided which will be the voice that will go on to the face on screen.

In this song, there was no such quandary.

I knew from the beginning, as the sur started unfolding, that this was Manna's song. Only he will give it the weight and the twist of mystery I want to invest it with.

Ralhan has explained the scene to me, I have asked in great detail, and he has filled in all the touches.

It is in a haweli, a music programme with a dancer performing. A classical dance, she is dressed in an apsara-like tight costume, like a sculpture.

The song is sung by a classical singer invited for the evening. He has accompanists.

The audience stands.

The hero, who is the host's partner, is also standing in front.

On one side, the host's daughter, Sharmila Tagore, is sitting. She is dressed in Western clothes, a bright blue dress I am told, and long white gloves. She has coloured lenses in her eyes.

The story is that she looks exactly like the village girl Rajendra Kumar, the hero, had fallen in love with a year ago and had promised to return to marry. Here, his partner wants him to marry this girl, who is also wooing Rajendra Kumar in a very open fashion, as Western girls do. And because she looks so similar to his love, he is attracted to her. Besides, his career and job are also hinged on his marrying her.

The song is a pivotal moment in the film, revealing his confusion, indecision.

Majrooh has written it so nicely, I am very pleased. And we are sure Manna will sing it in the recording as well as he has in our rehearsals.

But Ralhan, he wants Mukesh.

MUKESH! But why!

Mukesh will never be able to sing this song, not the way I want it.

His voice is good for plainer, simpler numbers, and for pathos. This is aggression, mystery, philosophy! It won't work.

I won't do it. I won't work in your picture, I told Ralhan. Bas!

I picked up my packet of paan and left.

Only one thought nags me. What will happen to all the other beautiful songs I have made for the film?

♫

Luckily for the film and the history of cinema music, O.P. Ralhan, producer–director of *Talash*, realized he had stepped too far. He had crossed the line and a senior composer like S.D. Burman was not the person to take it lightly. He tried to make amends almost immediately.

To no avail, though.

The composer would not meet him, not at his house, not at his own place, not in the studio. Nowhere. It was as if the composer had blacklisted Ralhan.

It had always been like that with S.D. Burman. He would never get angry, he was never heard raising his voice, never known to throw a tantrum. His patience and humility were exemplary in someone as senior and accomplished as he was. His track record of successes gave him every right to call the shots, but he was thoroughly professional. Only his music mattered, and in that he brooked no compromise.

It was always a matter of the song for him, never one of ego, and in music there was no going back once he made up his mind.

If he could not have his way, he would not bend. Rather, he would drop all interaction with the person. Like a child at war!

Of course, there were times when his anger would peter out, like it did in his fallout with Shailendra. A lot depended on the other person.

This time, however, he seemed determined not to give in to even hear Ralhan out.

Weeks later, it would be his friend Vijay Anand who would persuade a reluctant Dada Burman to meet OP. And the large-hearted child that he was at the core, S.D. Burman accepted the profuse apologies offered by Ralhan and went back to the sets to complete his work on *Talash*.

Talash offered a bouquet of beautiful numbers that were typically Burman. The Lata-Rafi duet '*Palkhon ke peechhe se*' has a lovely story about it–narrated by the film's lyricist Majrooh Sultanpuri in an interview by Peeyush Sharma, courtesy Moti Lalwani–that tells of the composer's grit and dedication to perfection:

> *Talash* was another of the films we did together. It had the duet '*Palkhon ke peechhe se kya tum ne keh dala*', by Rafi sahab and Lata-ji. Dada had wanted Rafi to hum a tune just before he starts singing his line... Just how many times the humming should precede the line and how Rafi Sahab should hum it each time, this took almost four days to finalize and perfect. He was a perfectionist. He looked into all the details meticulously.
>
> Let alone recording his songs, no one else could create music the way he did. So any talk of someone else taking over his songs and composing them for him, or even changing them during recording is just empty talk, baseless rumour. There was no way.

Talash also had S.D. Burman singing the evocative '*Meri duniya hai maa*' through the film's titles while the background scene establishes the adoring love between Rajendra Kumar and his sick mother. Though in typical SD style, it is not one of his more popular numbers.

In an interview with Moti Lalwani and Richa Lakhanpal, Zarine Sharma adds a note on how instrumentalists were given a free hand to show their skill, adding depth and beauty to the music composed. In this perhaps, S.D. Burman followed the norm of Hindustani classical music, where the instrumentalist is allowed to express himself within the limits of the raga and the taal in any manner he chooses.

'I was called for,' she says of her first encounter with S.D. Burman's music. 'I was told that Dada has said that he was planning a rehearsal. I went for the rehearsal, and he sang the song for me, he made me listen to the song. The song was "*Tere naina talash*". And then the music was composed. Then he said, "This is the thing I have composed. Then there is this place in the music that I have left ... for you to create something to play." So then I played some thing to add to the song at that point. I asked him afterwards, "Dada, if I play it like this, will it be all right?"

'He said, "Yes, yes, it will be all right, it is good, very nice. Remember this; you have to come for recording."

'We rehearsed for one or two days, and then the recording was done as scheduled. Basu-da, his arranger, had meanwhile noted the exact tune I played, immediately after I finished playing it. And he checked it out with his notations when I played at the recording. I am sad that I hardly got to play much for him, though I played a lot for his son, Pancham. We did a lot of work together.'

74

It is true what Kaifi wrote. Everyone goes, leaving one behind. *Bichde sabhi bari bari…*

Sahir, Shailendra … where are you lost, my friends, poets who gave my songs words like gems, studded each note with jewels?

And my friend Majrooh … he is so busy, so busy, I don't see him any more. He is writing like a machine, and there is no time in his life now for his friend, Burman Dada.

Dev wants me to make a film. A new one, he is directing it.

I sometimes ask myself, should Dev direct his own film? He is handsome, very good looking, and the public loves him. But is he a director like Goldie?

I say nothing when he comes though. I listen. He talks. The film is called *Prem Pujari*. He will act in it, but naturally. But, he will also direct it. That is not so natural, not for him. I laugh at my own joke, playing with words. But my heart is sad. When I think of my new film, I miss my friends. Who will write my songs for *Prem Pujari*? Will the lack of good words make my music lose its lustre? Who will write like Shailendra, or Majrooh, or Sahir?

Dev is bringing someone new. Let me see. I miss my friends so much.

♫

Picture the poet at his task. Bent over the wooden table, light from his lamp spilling over the waves of his hair, his brow deeply creased by the burden of thought.

The composer has explained the scene to him. In great

detail. Explained too that there are some conceits that he finds abhorrent. No allusions to liquor, and all the other props that poetry usually cobbles together when the poet runs out of inspiration.

It would be the second time such a scene was being played out. Not so long ago, another poet, an unwilling one at that, had sat through the night thinking up images to suit the scene where a girl steals out for a glimpse of her lover despite the brightness of a moonlit night. Gulzar had passed the test, then.

And now it was this poet's turn.

Neeraj, for that was the poet's name, was not too worried. In fact, the clarity of the scene and the fact that the composer had decided he wanted the words 'rangeela re' to open the song, had made things quite simple. And yet, he toiled over the song, to fit the words into the tune, to make the emotions sound true.

If he failed, it would be the end of a dream. The composer was known to be uncompromising about his music. Would he accept a song written by a poet who was more literary in his approach to poetry than film music required? Placing his pen on the table, the poet rose. Pacing the room, he closed his eyes momentarily, to picture the scene.

A hotel room, a crowd of well-dressed men and women, guests for some event. The hero and his companion, well dressed, playing host and hostess, perhaps. And then the song by the heroine. Dressed in a white sari, epitome of purity and Indianness, for there was a patriotism angle to the film. She sees the hero, her lover, with the other woman, decides to drink to be able to express her anguish, and does so, by way of song. The drink loosens her tongue, and in her agony, her body whips about in a frenzied, yet graceful dance. Waheeda herself had decided on what the steps of the dance would be, and S.D. Burman and Dev had set the beat and rhythm of the music based on that. The song would run its course and end in a climax of sorts, as she rushes out of the room…

The visual runs out, and Neeraj starts pacing the floor again. Reciting his lines to himself, to check if they fit.

They did indeed.

♫

In an interview to Moti Lalwani and Richa Lakhanpal, Neeraj recounts the scene that occurred on the morning he was to submit the song:

> Dev Saheb once again said, 'Do recite the lyrics to me first.'
>
> After listening to the lyrics, Dev Saheb was all praise and exclaimed, 'Neeraj, fantastic! I have never heard such lyrics before! What a beautiful song you have written. Wah! Wah! Wah! Wah!'
>
> He picked up the telephone and called up Dada Burman. 'You must hear his lyrics, what splendid words he has written.' Burman Saheb heard the song and was completely mesmerized. He was all praise.
>
> Next day, while I was sitting with Dada, Dev Saheb called and said, 'I am going to bring Neeraj with me.'
>
> Dada replied, 'He is already here, you come over.'
>
> Dev Saheb came over. Dada inquired as to where I was staying? 'Santa Cruz,' I replied. To which Dada said, 'My car will come there in the morning, every

morning the car will come at nine to fetch you. You come here and both of us will work together.'

I said fine, and the work started thereafter.

Neeraj found that the writer in him responded wonderfully to the fact that he had to fit his words into tunes. The song wrote itself to the music. To quote him on this:

> The difference is that poetry by itself is static writing (with no melody, but with rhythm). There is no music in it. And the tune has action (expression oriented) in it. On screen it is enacted upon. The tune has breaks (meaningful gaps) in it, and there is timing involved. I have written this song:
>
> 'Rang mein pighle sona,
> Ang se yun ras chalke,
> Jaise baje dhun koiyee,
> Raat mein halke-halke'
>
> See, Dada has given a gap here, this is the gap, understand?
>
> Poetry is serious, I am reciting and you are listening to it. There is no acting involved. In other words poetry has no acting in it.
>
> In cinema, the action is on the screen. If the audience does not follow, in case of a mistake, they can't ask the screen. That's why simple words can be easily remembered. '*Ae bhai, zara dekh ke chalo*', and '*Rangeela re*' can be easily recalled.
>
> Dada used to experiment with what others would not dare! For instance, the song '*Phoolon ke rang se,*

dil ki kalam se' starts with the antara (subsequent stanzas after mukhda), the mukhda (beginning) comes later!

'Phoolon ke rang se, dil ki kalam se, tujhko likhi roz paati,
Kaise bataaon, kis kis tarah se, pal-pal mujhe tu satati,
Tere hi sapne lekar ke soya, teri hi yaadon mein jaaga,
Tere khayalon men uljha raha yun, jaise ki mala mein dhaga,
Badal-bijli, chandan-paani, jaisa apna pyaar,
Lena hoga, janam hamein, kayee kayee baar'

And now here comes the mukhda:

'Itna madhir, Itna madhur, tera mera pyar…'

The mukhda is from here. You see, after six lines the mukhda begins.

Then Dada experimented further. 'I don't want mukhda. I don't want mukhda at all. And this he did in *Gambler* with:

'Dil aaj shair hai,
Gham aaj naghma hai,
Shab yeh ghazal hain sanam,
Gairon ke sheron ko o sunne wale,
Ho is taraf bhi karam…'

There is no mukhda in this song at all. This is pure poetry.

He further broke away from the existing trends, saying, 'Now Neeraj, in one mukhda, we will introduce four genres of music. First two lines would be based on folk, the third line will be based on classical, the fourth line on pop, the fifth line on qawwali.'

This is the song:

'Gham pe dhool dalo
Kahkaha lagalo
Arre kaanto ki dagariya, zindagaani hai
Tum jo muskara do, Rajdhani hai
Yeh honth sookhe sookhe, yeh baal rookhe rookhe,
Chhaayi udaasi kyon yaaron,
Arre yaaron neelaam karo susti, hum se udhaar lelo masti,
Arre hasti ka naam tandurusti.'

♫

Neeraj's songs in *Prem Pujari* would be counted among S.D. Burman's most poetic creations. Unfortunately, the songs were wasted gems. Dev, the actor, was not as skilled a director as his brothers.

Goldie's influence shows through in the filming of the Waheeda–Dev duet '*Shokhiyon mein ghola jaye*', where Waheeda is placed on a haystack much as she was in *Guide*, singing '*Kaaton se kheench ke yeh aanchal*'. The picturization of both '*Rangeela re*' and '*Phoolon ke rang se*' were also lacking in originality and depth. Waheeda's dance in half-drunken agony is a shadow of her spirited snake dance with echoes of '*Mose chhal*'. And for a song as ethereal as '*Phoolon ke rang se*', the visuals are thoroughly uninspired and mundane. In short, they matched the lacklustre directional mood of the rest of the film.

When he saw *Prem Pujari*, S.D. Burman moaned that the film lacked soul, that something just did not work for his songs either.

In fact, Waheeda has gone on record to recount how the composer, who often sat watching scenes being shot, told her after a long day at the studio that he was feeling very depressed.

After *Guide*, the work that was expected from you and Dev has not occurred, he told Waheeda, adding that there was a world of a difference in the quality of *Guide* and *Prem Pujari*. 'It does not work for me,' he continued, shaking his head sadly.

Waheeda asked him, 'You must have heard the story.'

Dada replied, he had, but that was before the shooting started, 'but now I am very depressed. Some of my really good songs have been wasted. You should have said something, why did you not,' he asked Waheeda, to which the actress responded saying, 'He is the director, the producer and I have known him so long ... what can I say to him.'

'All the more reason, since you know him for so long,' the composer had replied. Then, he repeated, 'No-no this isn't good, it is just not working, not working. My songs have been wasted.'

'And sadly that is exactly what happened,' Waheeda said, 'the picture flopped.'

Despite that, *Prem Pujari* would be remembered. For its songs. And Neeraj would go on record that of all the royalties he received for his compositions for films, the largest share came from his songs for S.D. Burman.

75

S.D. Burman's duets always had something offbeat in them. He would bring in natural exclamations that made the exchange between the singers seem more real, like the 'Aah' by Asha Bhonsle in '*Chhod do aanchal*'. In *Chalti ka Naam Gaadi* he had Kishore Kumar sing in numerous styles in one song, '*Paanch rupaiyya barah anna*'. In *Aradhana*'s playful duet filmed on Farida Jalal and Rajesh Khanna, Lata's 'na na na na' following the quizzing by Rafi added the perfect touch to the characters' moods and personalities. In fact, whatever the mood of the duet, be it playful, sad, or romantic, Dada Burman would manage to get it in perfect sync with the scene. And in the year he created the unmatchable tunes for *Talash* and *Prem Pujari*, he crafted one of his finest duets for a nondescript film, *Jyoti*.

Taking his cue from a Bangla composition by Himangshu Dutta, '*Chhilo chaand meghero parey*', which was in itself a complex mix of ragas – Malkauns, Jogia and Samanta from Carnatic music – which the composer had named Pushpachandrika, S.D. Burman changed the metre and gave it a new twist. Sung by Manna Dey and Lata, filmed as a softly romantic night scene bathed in moonlight, the song, '*Soch ke yeh gagan jhoome*', would be counted among Dada's best.

76

I was right, he thought, as he sat listening to the radio. The song came clear and loud over the air waves, and he smiled when he imagined his beloved Asha singing it, swaying slightly, as she articulated the words to the tune with her characteristic zest and gusto.

They had come to him with the film, Dev and his assistant. And he had refused. Point Blank. Take Pancham, he had said, smiling, but firm as a rock. Nothing would make him change his mind, and no, he would not hold the boy's hand or peer over his notations to see if he was doing the right thing. And now, the song was a rage. It was pure; it held the spirit of the film. He smiled and eased his slight body into the easy chair as his eyes took in a flower caught at the point of blooming. Like Pancham, he thought. The boy's time had come.

Dum maro dum
Mit jaye gham
Bolo subah shaam
Hare Krishna Hare Raam

It would be an exercise for music buffs and SD fans to imagine how the song would have shaped up in the maestro's hands.

If Dev Anand had had his way, S.D. Burman would indeed have spun out the tune, giving it possibly, knowing the setting, a north-eastern or pahadi flavour. There was no reason for Dev to imagine that his most trusted composer would turn down his request.

He had amazing powers of persuasion, Dev did; besides, his ebullience and energy were boundless and infectious. He was still drunk on the success of *Johnny Mera Naam* which quite eclipsed the failure of his first production. And riding the wave of this success, he crafted the idea of a film that would be as sensational in theme as it would be offbeat.

The 1970s was the era of the flower children. Drug addiction was sweeping through colleges and schools, and dropouts were leaving the cloistered security of their homes to exhale in the freedom of smoke-filled drug dens.

Always quick with responses to social issues, Dev Anand launched *Hare Rama Hare Krishna*, with a brother-sister theme at its centre, and a love angle thrown in for good measure. There was enough scope for good music, as in all Dev's films. And the double thrust would give the composer enough variety to play around with.

Despite media reports to the contrary, it was not Dev who chose Pancham for the film's musical score, but S.D. Burman who decided his son would handle the film.

For one, the elder Burman disapproved of drugs and the filming of such scenes. He was not sure of its impact. Besides, he felt someone younger would be more in tune with the kind of scene Dev would shoot and be able to fit the music in better.

H.Q. Chowdhury reports in his book that in a personal interview with him, Dev Anand spoke about the fact that he did request S.D. Burman to at least score the softer, more folk-based songs for the film, leaving the younger hippie numbers to Pancham.

But S.D. Burman, worried about the fact that his gifted son's career was not really flying as high as it should, and was floundering around like a kite with no wind to lift it off, suggested that Pancham should handle the film on his own. Maybe the disappointment with *Prem Pujari* and his understanding of Dev Anand's limited abilities as a director were at the back of his mind too, but in handing the entire film to his son, the maestro must have had only one thought in mind. He knew Pancham could handle all aspects with brilliance. He knew his son's measure of talent.

History proved him right. The title song, shot on a young, fresh Zeenat Aman, who burst into the viewers' consciousness with her role as Dev Anand's hippie sister and would in future films change the way heroines dressed and looked, was a runaway hit. Adopted as an anthem by the youth of that time, the song gained cult status. If *Teesri Manzil* had seemed a flash in the pan, *Hare Rama* proved beyond doubt that Pancham was a kite who would threaten his own father's space in the sky with daring and impunity.

For the father, it was a mixed blessing. On the one hand, his son was finding his own space. But on the other, he must have sensed that he would be left to manage a lot more on his own, with the boy who had first started assisting him as a teenager in *Pyaasa* no longer by his side in the studio.

Yet there was still time. The father would still have teachings that would stand the son in good measure. And add wind beneath his wings.

77

He dreams of being father to his son. Of taking forward what his father had done; a spool unwinding its thread of music through generations. Maybe his son will also be a musician, he thinks; then, in his sleep, he smiles.

The vision of a child on his lap, crumpling his spotless dhoti, comes uninvited. He watches the scene as if distanced from it, yet his heart swells. The child jumps off and sits on the ground. He sees himself approaching, up the step, to the door, and stopping as he hears the sound of the tabla. Who could be playing, he wonders as he pushes open the door. The child sits cross-legged, his small back ramrod straight, his eyes shut as his fingers, small and still plump, and his wrist encased in puppy fat, drum on the tabla. He laughs, and runs across to pick the boy up.

Again, watching the scene his heart swells.

Unspoken desires, his lips mumble, and the child vanishes, the scene dissolves.

Restless now, he cannot sleep. Thoughts crowd into his head, jostling each other like they were riding an overflowing train to the land of grief. And his heart contracts.

He must seek recourse in happier thoughts.

Far away the sound of the song comes to him, uncurling into his consciousness, a smoke of memory with its own set of images.

Only a few months ago, he had been creating the song … sat listening to the boy trying to shape it. Lata standing by, as Pancham played out the tune. A bhajan, it was sweet and melodic.

But he had been disturbed; it was too staid, too pat. Something had to make it different, or it would be just another song. The boy could do better than this!

It was perhaps his last real lesson. The re-tuning of the song '*Bada natkhat hai re*' that was now swirling around the room he lay in.

'Listen, can you hear that?' Meera's voice floated in from the room, but he did not quite hear it, nor notice the marked pride in her voice. If he had, he might have stopped to wonder if the same pride bordered her voice when she spoke of his music to others.

But his mind was elsewhere. He was caught in the bubble of memory. His sitting with Pancham. His telling him to change the song.

The song being filmed on Sharmila, who was chasing a playful child, not her own. The director had wanted a bhajan. It would remind the audience of the love of Yashodha for the infant Krishna, who was not born from her womb, but was still her son. The relationship in the film was similar,

The child saw Sharmila as his mother, though she was not.

The boy had created the bhajan all right. But he, the father, was not happy with what he heard. No, it would not do. He had told his son so. Where is the emotion in the song, where is the mother's love, the overflowing of unconditional love, the laughter at his mischief, the worry over his future. All of it should spill out of the song in layers, as the tune unfolds. He had said as much, and the boy and the director had listened with gravity.

Going a step further, he had taken the tune and embellished it with twists ... a shift here and there, an emphasis on a word, and suddenly the song was alive. It was no longer a bhajan, but so much more. It would cause women to sigh and weep, and also take the story forward.

He had watched Pancham's face light up as the song was played in its changed form. It was his tune all right, but changed masterfully!

He had patted the boy on his shoulder and left the room.

Amar Prem, that is the love a father has for his son, regardless of who he is, what he does, what he becomes in life.

His son had become a composer after all, and one now chased by producers.

But while finding peace in one quarter, he had lost it in another. Jet was not a home any more. The room across his was empty, there were no sounds floating through the door. The music hall was silent when he was silent, there was no Pancham trying out his tune, or playing his instruments.

The last time, the boy had sat with a glass of liquid, swirling it, swirling the spoon in it, listening to the sound of the liquid against the glass. He had taken a comb and run it against the glass. He had watched indulgently and a bit mystified by the boy's strange obsession with sounds.

Now, everything was silent.

Meera broke into his mood. 'What music, what a song,' she said, as she entered, wiping her hands on the edge of her sari. 'You should be proud of the boy.'

He sat up. Proud he was, but this emptiness…

'I am,' he responded, 'I am.'

And he lay down on his bed, and turned to face the wall.

Every living creature does the same, he consoled himself. It is nature's way. How often had he looked out of his window to see the birds being taught to fly? Small sorties, then larger circles, then out into the sky. How patiently the parent would teach, lead, follow, keeping an eye out for a marauding hawk or kite. Within a week, the nest would be empty, the little ones would have flown away, maybe to make nest of their own, have their own babies to teach.

Each generation must make its own nests, he mused, but the heat behind his closed lids would not cool. I have to come to terms with this, he said, the boy is only a road's length away. And visits often. Besides, he is doing what I dreamt of for him, making good music and earning a big name.

How proud he had been, when coming across some young people during his walk he had overheard them saying he was the composer R.D. Burman's father. Today, more listeners tuned in to Paṇcham than to him; if there was ever a contest on popularity, the boy would win. There was joy in that.

But he was lonely. There was no denying that. Or getting away from it, either.

78

Meghaa chhaae aadhi raat, bairan bann gai nindiyaa
Bataa de mai kyaa karun…

Sab ke aangan diyaa jale re, more aangan jiyaa
Hawa laage shool jaisi, taanaa maare chunariyaa
Kaise kahun mai mann ki baat, bairan bann gayi nindiyaa

That, he thought, as he listened to the song after recording it, is exactly how I feel. *Sab ke aagan diyaa jale re, more aagan jiyaa.* It was as if Kavi Neeraj had entered his heart and read the sorrow seated there. A wordless, unspoken sadness. With Pancham moving out, the chatter of the younger artistes had stilled, there was a quiet now that had the taste of solemnity, the musicians playing obediently, the arrangers seriously going about their work. They were overawed in his presence, he was the Karta, the guru. No mischief, no laughter, which though sometimes aimed at him by the youngsters, with Hari and Pancham ganging up to giggle surreptitiously, was still ebullient and pleasant. He missed it all.

The song swept into his thoughts, it was indeed beautiful, some of his sorrow had seeped into the notes.

He had watched the scene's progress, heard every nuance. Shashi Kapoor was romancing the heroine, the westernized one, who wore Western clothes, and was daring and teasing in her nature. And the other side of the coin was the twin, the wrong sister married to Shashi Kapoor, ignored by him, lamenting her loveless state.

He had worked the music well, blending the Western for the sister with Shashi and changing to sitar and tabla for the sorrowing twin. Though he felt that Western music was not really suited to Indian films – they were to him an exotic bloom that would quickly die or lose flavour in Indian minds – he knew how to use their instruments. They had their own place in creating mood and evoking the notes he wanted.

He had taken the strains of a Rabindra Sangeet song as the base. And used the bongo, guitar, drum and accordion to create a semblance of faster, lighter pace. When he moved to the classical sitar and tabla combination in the mukhdas, the pace seemed more majestic, slower ... in keeping with Neeraj's lyrics that in pure Hindi best delineated the heroine's tearful mood, and measured, as if, the pace of her steps.

The songs of *Sharmilee* would all be hits, he was sure of that. They would all be remembered years from now. But in this number, he knew he had a winner. One etched from his heart.

79

The Citadel was a 1938 film made in black and white which boasted of some of the brightest luminaries of Hollywood. Directed by King Vidor, the film was based on a novel of the same name by A.J. Cronin, and starred Robert Donat, Rosalind Russell, Ralph Richardson and Rex Harrison. It went on to win three Oscars: for best picture, best director and for best actor.

Director Vijay Anand decided to remake A.J. Cronin's story of the young zealous doctor who is corrupted by money only to find his way back to his vocation and win back the respect of his wife. Dev Anand would produce the film under the Navketan banner.

Dev Anand was of course to play the young doctor; Mumtaz was signed on as the heroine, and Vijay Anand himself had taken on the role that Ralph Richardson had played in the original.

The film was to be shot in the hilly outback of Chindwara and Parasia, where mustard fields dotted the undulating landscape. And there were also coal mines that formed the backbone of the early half of the story. The yellow flowering fields would form a great backdrop for romance and music, against which would unfold one of the most romantic songs of Hindi cinema, '*Maine kasam li*', with the hero and heroine cycling through narrow roads winding their way through fields dotted with golden flowers. The coal mines, on the other hand, would take the story forward, giving the characters credibility, and a setting suitable to the plot.

S.D. Burman was, as expected, in charge of the music.

Adding the Indian touch to the sparse, tight story of the original, the director expanded the role of the livewire, hysteria-prone millionaire in the original to the status of a second heroine, played by Hema Malini. A dancer, she gave the director scope to film scenes with theatre-style dances and sets to match.

As in many of his earlier films, S.D. Burman had two women to compose songs for, each set against a different backdrop, yet linked to the hero in definite ways.

The music composer would make capital of the opportunity. Hema's songs, '*Tha thai*' and '*Udd chala*', would be foot tappers, holding in the tunes and lyrics the same light-as-air quality that Tanuja's song in *Jewel Thief* had done. Asha again proved that under S.D. Burman's baton she could let her voice soar to amazing heights of lightness.

But it was with the songs he composed for Mumtaz in *Tere Mere Sapne* that the maestro really struck gold.

The bhajan-like love song in which the music director combined the Bengal kirtan tradition with the bhajan was filmed evocatively by the director. He had Mumtaz wrap herself in a red dupatta that Dev has bought for her at the fair, and sing the words '*Jaise Radha ne mala japi Shyam ki, maine odhi chunariya tere naam ki*', while Dev watched through a window. It had all the makings of a classic.

And almost a precursor to the soft reawakening of hope in *Abhimaan* which would follow two years later, the hope-filled Kishore–Lata duet '*Jeevan ki bagiya mehekegi*' shone like a jewel among the compositions.

If the Jayshree T. village number '*Mera saajan phool kamal ka*', rendered by Asha was loud and noisy as suited to the scene, '*Mera antar ek mandir*' would make up in softness, regret and the ability it had to tinge deep love with pathos and a sense of loss.

And again, foretelling his semi-comic compositions that waited in the years ahead in films like *Chupke Chupke* and *Chhupa Rustam*, S.D. Burman had Manna De sing '*Zamane dhat tere ki*'.

♫

Tere Mere Sapne was in another way an indication of times to come.

The songs were almost done, just the background score and one duet was remaining, when suddenly, the composer found his assistants and arrangers missing.

He knew where they were of course.

Manohari Singh said in an interview how during the shooting of *Tere Mere Sapne* most of the assistants were working for both father and son.

R.D. Burman was composing for Gemini Films' *Lakhon Mein Ek* and the background score, which remained, had to be completed and recorded in Madras. The Madras producers would not wait, and R.D. Burman rushed with his assistants and musicians to Madras. Manohari and Basu Chakravarty among them.

Of course it upset the senior Burman.

How can you leave my work and go away, he asked Manohari, and perhaps for the first time ever, Manohari heard an edge of anger in his voice.

He was justified, of course, Singh added. He was old school, and believed in professionalism and commitment. And there was just one shift left to complete his film. I shall not call you again, he said, and that was that.

However, Singh added that the anger was soon forgotten. 'He was fine with us after that. He respected us a lot, even when he was just talking to us, one could see that.'

The senior Burman did call the arrangers for one or two songs after this episode, for *Barood*.

And then there was nothing.

Adding the other piece of this story is the narration by Pandit Shiv Kumar Sharma who remembers that Dada Burman called him and Hari Prasad Chaurasia to work on a song. He gave them the song '*Jeevan ki bagiya mehekegi*', and told them, 'I do not want any arranger, just want the two of you to play whatever you like.'

He explained the scene. 'She's expecting and they are celebrating … that is the mood. And I will not use any arranger for this song. What you two play, that will be the final arrangement for the song.'

'Listen to the song and you will hear mainly the santoor and the flute,' Shiv Kumar adds.

That is how it was, just the two of them, and a tabla for rhythm.

'And he would sing the song for us, and we would immediately compose the pieces, and ask, Dada, is it okay, should we move to the second antara. He'd say, okay, and we would move on. The song got completed in this fashion.'

The composer never mentioned this to anybody.

'But it was his way of coping, of knowing that even if left bereft of his old companions, he would make his music.'

The tragedy, though, was that the songs sparkled but the film failed. Today, *Tere Mere Sapne* is recognized as a film with unmistakable Vijay Anand touches, but at that time, the audience was not excited by the story of a doctor who misplaces his idealism in his search for success, only to find it again! Like *Kaagaz ke Phool*, *Tere Mere Sapne* bombed because it dealt in abstracts, rather than black and white contrasts.

80

The Burman home kitchen. The cook's assistant is cutting vegetables, there is oil in a kadhai on the stove and the cook stands, hand on hip, looking down to see the progress. He adds the seasoning to the oil, the mustard and panch-phoran hiss and sputter and crackle, as he bends down to pick up the cut vegetables and prepares to add them to the oil.

He stirs the vegetables in, covers the vessel and turns to pick up the fish he has marinated and left on a thali. A maid comes in, she is humming a tune from *Tere Mere Sapne*.

Cook: Oof so much work, this never ends, day after day, all I do is cook.

Maid: Don't complain. You have grown used to being lazy when Ma used to cook. Now that she goes to the studio, you are complaining of too much work.

Cook: Not a day off this month. Not one moment to spare.

Maid: Chup. You eat well, you get to sleep in the afternoons.

The cook is busy with the fish.

Maid: O ma, I smell burning. Don't burn the vegetables, or ma will be very upset.

Cook *(rolls his eyes and shrugs)*: Upset! Have you heard her when she is upset? She is more pungent than the mustard oil! (*Mumbles.*) And anyway, when is she not upset?

Maid: Don't grumble. They are your bread and butter, just do your work.

Cook: Baap re, what do they feed you that you are so loyal?

Maid: Loyal? Where else can you get to hear such music day in and day out? It eases away my tiredness, it lifts my spirits. We don't need a radio in this house, Karta's music is enough.

Cook *(thoughtfully)*: That is true. But what about her? You call her shrieking music too? Her temper? She even shouts at *him* sometimes.

Maid *(nodding sadly)*: She does, but he is quiet, never gets angry. He only has his music, cares about nothing else. But yes, she must not get angry with him, he is a sadhu.

Cook: Since baba went, she has become louder, she shouts for no reason.

Maid: True. But you were not here when bou was living here. She made her life miserable. I tell you, if the young couple had lived elsewhere, they would still be married … I blame her … *(to herself)* And now, with him gone away too, Karta is so quiet, so quiet.

Cook: Let her shout at me, and I will pack up and go. Let her find someone else, or cook her own food. And make her own tea … and … *(He cuts savagely at the fish.)*

81

Meera Dev Burman was proving a perfect teammate to her husband. Trained in music herself, and an able writer of songs, she was now also the arranger and chief assistant, after her son's departure in search of his own pot of gold..

As if the additional responsibility of studio duties was an impetus, she wrote songs almost with a new fervour. It was as if she seized with both hands her chance to show that in a family of stars, she could shine just as bright as the others.

Or perhaps it was the tiny tract of land that had once belonged to Pakistan but now was an independent nation called Bangladesh that inspired her. The composition '*Tak dhum, tak dhum bajai Bangladesher dhol*' was almost an offering to Karta so he could salute the place of his birth as she shook off the shackles of an oppressive owner.

Resorting to a folk style that was common in the region, S.D. Burman composed the song in its native garb, but of course typically made what was a rustic slow tune into a song much more contemporary and acceptable by adding a faster tempo and a quicker rhythm.

Though Pancham was not always by his side now, and was creating his own niche in the world of films, though the father sometimes worried that his son, like Icarus, might fly too fast, too close to the sun of popular choice, sacrificing real music in the process, he must have found some joy in the new partnership ties that Meera, moving in to fill the void, forged with her husband.

82

As the Bengali folk numbers penned by Meera continued to run like a stream alongside the main river of his film compositions, the one seems to have had a real impact on the other.

S.D. Burman's tunes for the year 1971-72 for his Hindi songs were all based more strongly than before in the folk tradition. In *Yeh Gulistan Hamara*, he would evoke the high, shrill flute-like notes of the north-eastern folk songs, especially in the number by Lata, '*Kya yeh zindagi hai*'. It was a plaint written by Anand Bakshi, and in the chorus which provided a bass relief to the high notes, the juxtaposition of the rustic with the composer's innate sophistication is evident.

Yeh Gulistan Hamara ran side by side with *Zindagi Zindagi*, *Us Paar* and *Anuraag*. All of them would be characterized by a deep delving into his roots. They were good films, and good songs, but they somehow did not have the ability to evoke the adulation that his compositions for *Guide*, or even *Talash* or *Tere Mere Sapne* had. Also, the films were not in the same class either and as such their songs failed to travel. *Zindagi Zindagi* would win for him a National Award, but the songs would not remain on the airwaves with the same persistence that the songs of earlier films showed.

Time, and the changing tenor of his life, health problems and the fact that there were so many newer composers, among them his own son, pushing new ideas and rhythms that created new emotions and sound sequences, were all combining to form a backdrop of fatigue.

For a while it seemed that though he still toiled endlessly

in the service of his chosen Goddess of Music, Saraswati, the maestro was waning.

83

From Amitabh Bachchan's blog Day1061

And the time and energy spent with the creators of this eternal element in our lives is divine. Some of the most eloquent moments in my rather sketchy career with music have been with its creators.

The hours of absolute bliss spent in time with the maestro S.D. Burman as he sat cross-legged on the floor of his apartment on Link Road in a building called The JET! One would never associate JET with his calibre and genius. But there he was, his equally talented wife and mother of R.D. Burman by his side, singing in his unique quality of voice, the songs of *Abhimaan* – each one a melody that has lived beyond time and place! For his accompaniment a harmonium and that is all. The simplicity of the bearing, the intensity of his compositions in its rough, bare form and the purity of its rendition were unmatched.

Somehow, once you moved into the realm of technology and the recording studio that aura of its quality evaporated.

Yes, we documented it for posterity, but I doubt if those moments spent in his preparation were ever recorded and kept. A real pity! For those are the moments that truly demonstrate the creative genius of the greats. The Americans are exceptional in this. Perhaps the age of their country as a country has prompted them to do so, but they seem to have every bit of documentation of almost every moment in their history on record. From the early lives of Presidents to the most accomplished sportsmen and musicians and artists, they have it all. And what surprises me the most is how do they divine whether Michael Jordan or Babe Ruth or a Muhammad Ali in their teens would become what they did. Or an Elvis or a Brando or JFK and a Nixon or Obama. Amazing! Absolutely amazing!

But back to music and S.D. Burman and musical sittings with other greats – Kalyanji Anandji, Laxmikant Pyarelal, R.D. Burman and so many others … all those evenings spent in their music halls, just faffing and relaxed and then suddenly out of nowhere comes a piece and it is developed and put down and recorded and performed to and it becomes history in the annals of cinema.

What a long way we have come from the time when we had singing actors and actresses, who sang on set to a live orchestra. And those wonderfully exquisite footages we have seen in the archives, of the leading lady and the leading man, singing a duet in the opulence of a garden or a forest and as they moved and danced and sang, the live orchestra moved along with them just behind the camera, or if they were under a tree, to find the live orchestra sitting on top on the branches, violins drums cellos being played with equal dexterity. I think the much-repeated expression used cynically even in today's times of 'running round the tree' when criticizing our song and dance routines, came about from those early shooting experiences. If the leading man were to be under a tree, a not-too-undesirable location for romance, and his lady were to be on the other side of it, the mobile live orchestra had to quickly run around the tree to keep out of the frame, if the hero decided to reach out to his heroine on the other side with some rapidity! Ha ha ha! Those were the days!

I was narrating this to some of the younger generation stars on set one of these days and they all thought I was being ridiculously funny! Until they realized it was all factual.

♫

Amitabh Bachchan on Abhimaan *in* Mumbai Mirror, *'Roop Nagar, Prem Gali', by Indu Mirani in 11 October* 2009

This film was very special for Jaya and me because we had produced it.

Hrishi-da was our godfather. S.D. Burman saab gave the music and the time we spent with him during the music sittings was unforgettable. The way he'd sing we failed to bring the essence into our recording. I always felt that that there was some kami (lacking) somewhere, he would sing so beautifully. The song was shot in a village near Belgaum. Hrishi-da wanted a village environment with a small temple, a river, a sacred pond with its water capable of uniting two people in love. We found such a pond.

Back then, Jaya and I weren't married. It was very special time for both of us.

Jaya had long, ankle-length hair then.

♫

In 1977, Martin Scorsese would make a musical based on the musical compatibility but the personal incompatibility of a couple, who fall in love, but cannot make music together.

New York, New York, Scorsese's tribute to the musical films of an era before his time, teamed Robert De Niro in one of his career's most outstanding roles as a saxophone player.

Ego clashes, with De Niro's character unable to take his wife's success would be one of the factors that would drive them apart; his bad temper and lack of understanding and commitment, being the other.

The film, considered a classic of sorts today, failed, for a variety of reasons and allegedly drove the star director to drugs and depression.

Four years before *New York, New York*, Hrishikesh Mukherjee would make a film about a couple, brought together by the very music that later comes between them, as rivalry rears its head, and the husband finds he cannot quite take his wife's success.

Abhimaan was conceived as a musical. And the director, knowing how well S.D. Burman had tackled *Manzil*, approached the maestro to create the score.

Burman was pleased with the project; here was something he could really create to his heart's liking. Majrooh Sultanpuri is on record on how Dada picked up the phone and told Hrisihkesh Mukherjee "ke *Abhimaan* ke subject ke liye Majrooh hi theek hai", aur mujhe phone kar diya ke maine tumhaara naam bata diya hai, kal aa jao aur composing shuru karte hain' (Majrooh alone is worthy of this project, and then phoned the lyricist to tell him, 'I have given them your name, come tomorrow and we can start composing'). 'There was no question of countering his decision in such matters, no one in the industry would do it,' Majrooh adds.

Abhimaan recreated the mood of Dev Anand's 1960 film

Manzil for Dada. Here was a story, simple and pastoral, a village setting as one of its main backgrounds, offset by music studios and a home where both partners were singers.

Hrishikesh Mukherjee knew the theme would attract the composer. Perhaps that was the reason he chose S.D. Burman over Salil Chowdhury who had composed an unforgettable music score for *Anand*.

Hrishikesh Mukherjee's hunch proved correct. S.D. Burman grabbed the opportunity to give his genius full rein. 'Main aisa meetha kabhi nahin chhodoonga,' he reportedly said as he took on the film.

It would make cinematic history for both the producer as well as the music director. Fired by the unspoken competition between the husband and wife in the rendition of their music, S.D. Burman created songs that have remained unparalleled.

Keeping the classical base intact, the composer built a tower of popular music that beguiled the audience with its hummable simplicity. The film would necessitate the heroine slowly overshadowing her more successful husband, and S.D. Burman gave Lata haunting melodies that rose gradually in difficulty and melodic value. The pastoral '*Nadiya kinare*' introduced her as the singer who enchants the city-based singing idol, and from there, Jaya, playing the perfect foil to an Amitabh who was courting her off-screen and who she would soon marry, moved on to '*Ab to hai tumse*' and '*Piya bina*'.

Abhimaan went on to win for S.D. Burman his second Filmfare Award, twenty years after *Taxi Driver*. It was a long, long gap, and not really one that could be understood by his fans, who knew that in film after film he had served only the best compositions. *Pyaasa, Kaagaz Ke Phool, Bandini, Guide, Jewel Thief* and *Aradhana* were films that many thought should have bagged him the award without any doubt. Strangely enough, it was a fate he would share with his son, who never won the Filmfare Award despite compositions of the quality of *Teesri Manzil, Amar Prem, Kati Patang, Mere Jeevan Saathi, Aap Ki Kasam, Kinara, Aandhi, Yaadon Ki Baraat* that moved from the classical to the popular with remarkable felicity. He would win one as late as 1983 for *Sanam Teri Kasam*, at best a mediocre score when judged against what went unawarded.

Doubtless, by then SD cared little about the award; for him, each film was a gem to be set to show off its best sparkle, and each song was an offering at the altar of the goddess of learning and music. *Abhimaan* also won him the Sur Singar Samsad award for the maximum number of classical compositions in a film.

One question that remains unanswered for many is why S.D. Burman used Manhar's voice in the duet '*Loote koi man ka nagar*'. It sounds laboured in comparison with Lata's–or perhaps that was the reason, as the story demanded that the heroine overshadows her husband in her music. Though one explanation offered has been that Manhar's voice was meant to be dubbed over but was not! Which would have been very uncharacteristic of the demanding music director, and perhaps a sign of changing power balances in the industry!

84

'*Tere mere milan ki yeh raina*', the Lata-Kishore duet in *Abhimaan*, is a springboard for controversy. Inspired by a Rabindranath Tagore tune, it proved a hit. It provides an opportunity to quickly discuss the Tagore–Burman connection, and the poet laureate's influence on other music directors.

H.Q. Chowdhury shares his opinion on this matter:

> Rabindra Sangeet's '*Ekoda tumi priye*' (1917) in the strains of Kafi, '*Jodi tare nai chini go*' (1923) in Khamaj or Khambaj as is called in Bengal, '*Hey khoniker athithi*' (1925) in Bhairavi, '*Loho loho tuley loho*' (1925) and '*Rodon bhara ei basantey*' (1936) in the flavours of kirtan, have often been a subject of discussion amongst music lovers as these tend to have something common with the extremely popular Hindi hits, '*Jalte hai jiske liye*', '*Tere mere milan ki ye raina*', '*Jaye to jaye kahan*', '*Megha chhaye aadhi raat*' and '*Mera sundar sapna beet gaya*', all composed by Sachin Dev Burman for films.
>
> Whether the songs composed by Burman are inspired, sourced from the same material or plagiarized is food for thought, keeping in mind that the lines demarcating inspiration, application of a portion of a particular genre of songs and plagiarism are very clear.
>
> A great composer is one who returns to the opening line of a song with ease, style and flair. The opening line could be from a raga or a folk song, the snatch of any song or a tune that a composer senses in the gentle wind by the river, for example.

That being the case, we find songs of similar openings but while most get lost, some attain immortality, thanks to the progression of the songs and their return to the opening lines. This is the secret behind the resounding success of Sachin Dev Burman's Hindi songs in question. One just marvels at the progression of the songs and their return to the starting points. On the other hand, the corresponding Tagore numbers had failed during the poet's lifetime; the internal musical routes and the style of singing could not hold on to the listeners' mind.

In course of time, when Sachin Dev Burman's massive hits were identified with the Tagore numbers, mind you with respect to the opening lines or a stanza, the old Rabindra Sangeets were re-recorded albeit with modern approach (which in fact was more Burman like than the originals!) to find listeners' acceptability. This prompted Tagore 'bhakts' to label Sachin Dev Burman's 'gifts' as 'lifts'!

Again, when Naushad composed '*Man tarpat Hari darsan ko*' in Malkauns in *Baiju Bawra*, we accused him of a 'Tagore lift' as the song had a semblance with '*Anando dhara bohichey bhuboney*'. Again, when Rajesh Roshan composed his '*Chhukar mere manko*' in *Yaarana*, we said it was Tagore's '*Tomar holo shuru*', little realizing that Tagore's piece itself was a European take!

One Tagore–S.D. Burman song, however, is confusing. Both '*Se din dujone*' – composed by Tagore in 1927 while travelling by train from Bangkok to

> Penang and–Sachin Dev Burman's '*Nain diwane*' (sung by Suraiya in the film *Afsar* and composed in 1949) have a striking similarity throughout the song. Vishwa Bharati never objected to S.D. Burman's use of this tune. Does it therefore mean that the tune is a traditional one from where both Tagore and Dada Burman derived their music? Tagore sometimes used tunes 'as it is' and changed the lyrics as in the case of the Bangladesh national anthem, '*Amar sonar Bangla*'; so did S.D. Burman like '*Megh de paani de*' in *Guide* which of course sounds somewhat different from the original because of his gayaki.
>
> In other words, the songs of interest were the transcreations of Tagore, and Sachin Dev Burman tapped from common roots and in these cases, the former was not much of a success while the latter got through with flying colours.

Perhaps the biggest surprise for SD fans comes with a well-loved song from *Pyaasa*. One of the Parampara series of CDs which covers the Burmans, father and son, under the title 'Songs from Bengal' has a comprehensive list of songs that were influenced by Tagore and other Bengali composers. This list also mentions that '*Jaane woh kaise log*', sung by Hemant Kumar in *Pyaasa*, was set to a tune inspired by '*Jana Gana Mana*', the Indian national anthem composed by Rabindranath Tagore. And verily, at least the first few lines seem to run quite close in both compositions.

Composer Shantanu Moitra (*Parineeta*, *3 Idiots*), in an interview to Moti Lalwani, has another take on S.D. Burman's adaptation from his own originals in Bangla:

> You know the structuring of his tunes from Bengali to Hindi was remarkably different. That's called weightage, down to structuring. Let's say: '*Borne gondhe chhonde geetite, hridoye diyechho dola*' … now look at the weightage of this, 1, 2, 3, 1, 2, 3 … For the same tune when it is in Hindi, he changed the weightage of the line '*Phoolon ke rang se*' (*Prem Pujari*, 1970). It is not in slow motion, like the original Bangla song, 'Phoo-lon-ke-ra-ng-se', he's not doing that, he is not slowing it down or dragging it out as in the Bangla version. He is doing, '*Phoolon ke rang se, dil ki kalam se*' at normal tempo.
>
> You can never make out, looking at that song, that it's taken from some Bengali tune. It's an original Hindi song. That is because he was a master of adapting a tune from one to another, and his own tune. But he was so sensible he knew that in Bengali I need that kind of a jhalak.
>
> The whole sensibility is completely different! It comes from a man who is an astute observer of people, an astute observer of music, with an astute understanding of what each language demands.
>
> What is happening today is that we are not concentrating; we think folk music boring hai, kaun lega, kya hoga, chalega ki nahin chalega. It's not just that. You have to know how to adapt that brilliantly. And I have done that, I have done that! I have used his philosophy in *Parineeta* (2005).

'Kasto mazza hai rail laima' – now this is folk! But *'Yeh hawayein, gungunaein, poochhe tu hai kahan'* – this was my line, I went after the folk!

S.D. Burman is so, so important for the youth of today, because the techniques that he used are important for composers like us, to make folk popular and to make it relevant.

85

He was worried. All evening he had tried to push off the thought, but it would not leave him. One day left for the recording and he worried it would not happen.

Why did the boy have to be so active? Running about like a rabbit, from one place to another, one city to another, taking planes and driving dusty distances.

There would be so much change in temperature, hot and cold, and sometimes wet. What it could do to the throat! To the voice!

And those numerous performances, without a chance to rest the voice…

Belting out songs, sad ones, soft ones, loud noisy numbers, changing pitch to suit the song … how could any voice, however gifted, bear the strain?

The recording room would be the acid test. And he worried that Kishore would fail the test.

He shook his head, and lay down to sleep.

Within minutes he was up. He could not rest.

What is it, Meera asked, but he would not answer. What is it?

Nothing, you sleep, he said, it will go away.

What will go away, she asked, half to herself, why is he like a rabbit, jumping out of bed and hopping about anxiously?

But he moved out of the room to pace the hall, and she sighed and kept her question to herself.

It would be a bad night, the hours would not move, if he waited on his resolve. He had to act now.

He had hit upon a solution, a way to find an answer to the question that irked him, and it would not wait till morning.

He would have to know now if his fears were grounded in reality or not.

He dialled the number, the phone rang and rang.

Finally, 'Hullo.'

He held the instrument closer to his ear, held his breath and listened.

Again, 'Hullo…'

The voice at the other end was clear.

He sighed, smiled and quietly replaced the receiver.

A while later, when dread seized him again, he dialled the number once more.

'Hullo,' Kishore Kumar's voice rang out, loud and clear.

'Aha, Kishore, you will come for recording tomorrow, yes?' he said, his own voice childlike with excitement and relief.

'Yes, Dada, I will.' Loud and clear again.

'Very good,' he responded and put down the receiver.

He could have danced a jig, but he restrained himself. The recording would go off on schedule, and go off wonderfully!

♫

In fact, Anandji adds in an interview by Moti Lalwani and Richa Lakhanpal that he would decide much beforehand when he wanted to record a particular song. He would pick up the phone and ring a singer–it could be Kishore Kumar, or Lata, or Rafi.

'How will your voice be in December?' he would ask, while it was still September or October. They would invariably answer, 'It will be fine. Dada.'

'Will it be fine for six months from now?'

'Yes, Dada.'

Now, you see, he knew these were busy singers, they recorded three, even four songs a day. He wanted their voices to be clean and fresh for his recordings.

He would say, I need you for a song, could be for one to ten minutes ... it could be any day, I will tell you. But on that day, don't take any other recording, don't sing for anyone else, I want your voice like that, open and fresh.

'He was that sort of composer, very particular,' Anandji says.

86

The years after *Abhimaan* were comparatively lacklustre.

Songs that come to mind as gems worthy of the maestro are the amazing duet by rivals Kishore Kumar and Rafi, '*Sa re ga ma*' in *Chupke Chupke*, Kishore's comic '*Dheere se jana khatiyan mein*' parody in *Chhupa Rustam*, and Lata's beautiful Holi number in *Phagun*, '*Piya sang khelo Holi*'. Though of the films that followed *Abhimaan* it would be Hrishikesh Mukherjee's *Chupke Chupke* that would show the spark still burning bright, it would be the director's *Mili*, the story of *Anand* with a female protagonist, that would find Dada Burman in full form again. But *Mili* would be a sad story in more ways than one.

87

What a poem Yogesh had composed.

He was more than moved by the note of sadness in it, the searing quality of loneliness the words expressed.

Badi sooni sooni hai…

The tune was heart-wrenching enough, but the words truly imbued it with a soul. Wah, Yogesh, he said, you have excelled yourself. I tell you, this song will be an eternal plaint for the lonely soul.

Sometimes he felt the same loneliness. He wondered why, but he knew the answer. He would never let it come to his mind and present itself. Enough then, to let it spin itself out in a tune.

Kishore will sing this song, he told himself, coming to a sudden decision … it was good also for Mukesh's voice, with its border of sadness, but Kishore would be the right voice for it.

He would sing it to him and see the reaction. It was his favourite ploy, to watch the reaction of the singer he had chosen, as he put the song out for the first time, words and music, and let it play to the very voice that would record it.

It helped them catch the nuances he wanted. And secretly, impishly, he knew he could bring to his tune much more than most of them could, though their voices were clearer, sharper, more acceptable to the listener when on screen.

As expected, Kishore listened attentively.

He was pleased. He was old now, and got tired easily, and happy that the boy did not bounce about and play his pranks as he used to do earlier. He sat sedate and listened.

A bit too quiet, he thought, does he not like the tune.

He sang, he finished singing. And waited.

The boy would not look up; he sat with his head bent over his knees.

Kishore, he asked, what happened?

When Kishore looked up, he was surprised to see his eyes full of tears!

He had made him cry! This laughing, joking child was crying to this tune of loneliness!

What chord in his heart had the song touched?

Kishore got up suddenly. I am going, he said, and before he could remonstrate, I am going and I will come back. When this song is ready, I will come back.

'Jab tak main ready nahin hoonga, yeh gaana record nahin hoga.'

He could only stare in silence at the space Kishore had occupied. He had left as if in a hurry. He knew the singer would work on the song, as was his habit.

He would send a recording with Yogesh for him to work on.

88

Meera sits by herself, thinking.

My eyes fill up, and I do not want him to see it. I turn away, swiping the edge of my sari against them, swiftly, in one quick movement.

It hurts me to see him sitting thus.

I know his soul aches inside his body, trying to tell it to move. It is captive, helpless. He wants and he cannot get.

Bablu is talking, I hear it but do not listen. My mind hears the soul fluttering inside, beating against his inability like a bird stuck in a room, hitting helpless wings against doors and windows.

They will all come, he says, all of them.

Karta is listening. Sitting ramrod straight. His eyes look not at Bablu but ahead of him, straight into the distance. Does he hear the words Bablu is speaking or the music of the song? Who can tell? He is so quiet these days, hurting because he cannot live with his music.

Anil, Arjun, Basu-ji, Manohari-ji, Maruti-ji and Ashish are all coming, Bablu is saying.

I think back on the list of arrangers, of Karta's team of musicians who have stood by him, learnt from him, created with him. Like a flock of migratory birds they flew away one by one. I look at Bablu. You too will fly away, I think, he is old, he is sick. Why will you stay, when you can find work elsewhere in a space now teeming with composers?

'Jethi-ma… it is correct, is it not?' He is addressing me. I turn my face to him and ask what is it? Sorry, I was not listening.

Bablu looks at me; he must see the pain in my eyes, because his voice goes soft. The bubbling excitement goes quiet.

'Jethi-ma, I was saying that though Dada is not coming for the recording, he need not worry. All his best musicians will be there. I have asked each of them personally, gone to their house and made the request. And they have agreed to come. And I will do the arranging, the best arranging I have done till today! I am telling you because Jethai is not saying anything. Tomorrow, Manohari will play the flute, Anil will play the violin, Arun will play the vibraphone. Bhupinder too has promised to come and play his twelve-string guitar.'

Suddenly, Karta speaks, his eyes are bright now, not glazed. I move towards him, but he is focused on Bablu. 'Basu will come?' he asks, and Bablu says, 'Yes, Basu Chakravarty will also come, and play the cello.'

He sighs, Karta sighs, Basu was always his favourite. Karta cocks his head a little, and looks at Bablu. He looks pleased.

'How, how did it happen,' he asks, softly. Like he is asking himself.

Bablu is bubbling now again.

'I went to all their houses. You know, Jethi-ma,' he says, looking at me, 'you know I have no fight or trouble with anyone. All of them love me, I may not be the best player, but they love me for who I am. So when I went and requested them to come, said it is my humble request, let us all play together for this song, come for this recording, you must come! They said yes. They will all be there. For your sake, for all you have done together.'

For all they have done together.

Karta sighs. Smiles. His face is pink with happiness.

Badi sooni sooni hai, says the song, but here everything is joyous.

I want to bless Bablu.

Kishore is sitting by Karta's side, listening quietly. He says nothing. But he must be relieved.

Tomorrow at the recording, he is in good hands. The best!

89

By the time the song was recorded, however, the composer was not well enough to be present. The musicians requested Pancham to handle the balancing of rhythm, orchestra etc., a tough job they felt only he could do justice to, to keep the song's purity intact.

Shantanu Moitra adds:

> S.D. Burman had of course instructed Kishore Kumar. You go, he had said, and theek theek gao, and, as Kishore Kumar was himself a composer, told him to keep an ear open on the music arrangement, and ensure it was fine.
>
> The song was recorded, and he carried the recording that evening to the composer, and then it was discovered that Kishore Kumar had sung it an octave higher than intended. Burman of course got very upset, such things made him angry and upset. He rebuked Kishore Kumar ... what sort of a singer are you, could you not realize you were singing it in the wrong sur? Kishore re-recorded the song. Beautifully.
>
> I do believe that as he sang, Kishore Kumar knew that Dada would not live very long after this period, maybe that brings that special pathos to his voice.

90

O re maajhi, o re maajhi, o o mere maajhi
Mere saajan hain us paar, main man maar, hoon is paar
O mere maajhi, abki baar, le chal paar, le chal paar…

There is a smell … a strange smell, what is it? Sickness?

There is a sound … a strange sound … what is it … soundlessness? Or do I hear the hiss of a breath drawn sharply in. Whose? Perhaps it is mine.

I feel something. An impediment. My throat is choked.

My body hurts, heavy. Like a stone on the river.

Far away, the boatman sings.

The waters ripple, the sun like a cloth of silver, no it is the moon, shining with golden light on the water. The boat slides over the silk, the cloth of gold ripples. The breeze disturbs the dragonflies, they lift their wings and fly among the reeds.

The boatman sings. It is my song he sings. I want to sing with him, blend my voice to his. I hear nothing, my voice is quiet.

I shall let the song lull me to sleep, fold away the disquiet rising from the thoughts that come like ripples to my mind.

The recording … it was like the sound of waves, they were all there. The red light … am I in the music room, surely that is the red light that shines close to me here. Is the recording on?

Meera is holding the floor, I can see her, though I know I am not there. Where is Pancham … why is he not here? There he is, naughty boy, peering from behind his grandmother's sari.

The boatman is louder, how is he here, here in the studio? Now I can hear the flute, how sweet it plays. Play on, flute, you remind me of my boyhood days.

Here in the sand my father's footsteps, I am walking carefully, putting my feet where his were, but my feet are smaller, slim and delicate; my feet never grew the way his did, they were royal feet. Father, wait for me…

Someone is talking, talking, I can hear the words like the rush of water over stones. What do they say? Who is talking?

I can hear crying. Meera crying? Meera never cries. She did not cry when Pancham went away, when the others went away. She is strong, stronger than I am. Meera crying … I want to get up, to open my eyes. Have I done that…

There is a commotion, his hand moved … hand moved … hand moved … ripples of sound, the silken water moves in silver moonlight. Is that my father who stands in the shadow, or my brother? I can't see clearly, the moonlight is too bright on the water.

Whose hand moved? God's? What is so wonderful about a hand moving?

And now there is silence … And I can hear the boatman singing … or is it Madhav…

What is it, what…

That is Pancham's voice, so clear. He is telling me, telling me, telling…

Everybody tells me something always, I hear nothing. Only the boatman sings again. My song.

They are calling. Dev wants a song, Guru is whistling my tune … who should I heed first.

I have sneaked away. They can't guess where I am, or maybe

they know and are letting me have fun. Today is a happy day, East Bengal is hammering Mohun Bagan … 5-0. They will lift the shield.

Rafi and Kishore … my first and second serves … they are singing a duet to celebrate … I can make out the words … they are singing Nazrul … am I hearing things? Geeta is singing too, over a phone? Where is Lata? Lata … There is too much noise. The crowd is celebrating.

It shines in my eyes, the light of the shield, the roar of voices in my ears … he smiled … smiled, smiling … smiled.

Of course I smiled. What is so great about my smiling when my team wins? I can sing and dance too, only the coils in my brain are so heavy…

Baba, Baba, Pancham calling from afar … he does not live with me anymore … he is planning to marry, he says. She said … who said … I cannot remember. But there will be songs many songs…

Baba…

Silence…

♫

S.D. Burman suffered a stroke soon after instructing Kishore Kumar how to sing 'Badi sooni sooni hai', and lay in coma for almost a year, with only one or two occasions when he showed some sign of awareness.

The composer passed away on 31 October 1975.

His music plays on.

AFTERWORD

Sachin Dev Burman: The Man behind the Legend

Moti Lalwani

The early 1950s. A group of us youngsters would escape to go and see a movie. We had to save our pocket money to buy a ticket costing five annas, and a couple more annas for a soft drink and a snack.

Our heroes then were Dilip Kumar, Raj Kapoor and Dev Anand. We enjoyed listening to Hindi film music, but there was something about the music of Dev Anand's films *Baazi*, *Sazaa*, *Jaal*, *Armaan* and *Taxi Driver*, which attracted us with its freshness, youthfulness and diversity.

By the time *Taxi Driver* was released in 1954, we had become lifelong fans of the peerless maestro who continued rewarding us with his unmatched and incomparable songs of different genres. Dev Anand's movies continued to project his youthful image through *House No 44*, *Munimji*, *Funtoosh*, *Paying Guest*, *Nau Do Gyarah*, *Kala Pani* and *Solva Saal* in the 1950s. The music was unbelievably enchanting even for die-hard S.D. Burman fans like us.

Initially, Kishore Kumar was the chosen singer for Dev

Anand, becoming one of the most popular singers of the time. The era of impish and romantic songs started with S.D. Burman, whose music helped Dev Anand build his image as a flirtatious, dashing and debonair hero, placing him as one of the top three leading stars.

Thanks to SDB's music, young girls fell in love with Dev Anand. The craze didn't even spare boys. A young man we knew bought a hat and a scarf and even got one tooth extracted to resemble his favourite hero. I did not go to such lengths, but as far as his music was concerned, I was as devoted a fan as any. We learnt much later that our idol, S.D. Burman, was a blue-blooded prince who had renounced his luxuries to pursue his passion for music.

Also in the 1950s, besides composing romantic songs for Dev, Dada composed music for serious films like *Devdas*, *Pyaasa* and *Sujata*, as well as comedies like *Chalti Ka Naam Gaadi*, with genres of music more varied than the hues of a rainbow! We continued to be rewarded with soulful music, year after year.

SDB was to move away from Kishore to Rafi (1957); and Lata to Asha (1958), as his prime singers. He moved back to Lata from *Bandini* (1963); and to Kishore from *Guide* (1965). Even though his assistants kept changing, his music always remained fresh and melodious.

Eventually, our group too split up, losing contact with each other as we grew up, each busy with his/her own career. However, I remained dedicated to Burman-da, eagerly awaiting new film releases featuring his music.

I started collecting published articles on SDB, not knowing that one day they would be handed over for this book. The collection increased with time, new friends adding to it, knowing my enthusiasm. There were no books in English on SDB, and there was no Internet back then.

♫

Once on Juhu beach in Mumbai, a young and pretty American lady in a meditative trance told actor Balraj Sahni and writer Vishwamitra Adil that she was inspired by the vision of a 'Buddhist Monk' who always appeared meditative while walking, as if in communion with God. 'Here he comes,' she said pointing to Dada Burman, who declared, 'Thinking of music and communion with God is the same thing!' No wonder then that he is fondly called 'Old Monk' by some of his ardent fans.

The simplicity of his tunes, loved by the common man as well as the connoisseur of music, is the reason his songs have enjoyed mass appeal all these years. A composer who used minimum instruments to create maximum melody, he was equally at ease handling a large orchestra if the situation so demanded.

J.V. Acharya, eighty-five-year-old sitar player, told us that while other composers used fifty to seventy-five musicians for the background music, Dada Burman used only one sitar in *Kala Pani* (1958), along with the sound of the printing press in the climax scene. When Acharya protested, saying, 'Dada, *mera ek sitar kya karega?*', Dada asked him to play *jhamm-jhamma*, decreasing the press sound and increasing the volume of sitar music.

Similarly, in *Bandini* (1963), for a particular scene when Nutan is shown running through the trees, arranger Anthony

Gonsalves had created exotic music which was rejected by Dada who created the background music with the help of a single flute. He asked the flautist Kamal Mitra not to play the flute, but to create a sound of vacuum by repeatedly inserting and withdrawing his finger on the non-playing side of the flute. There are many such instances where innovation was supreme.

At the same time, he didn't shy away from using Western tunes whenever necessary. As early as the 1950s, *Naujawan*, *Baazi*, *Bahar*, *Jaal*, *Taxi Driver*, *Pyaasa* and *Sujata* among others, demonstrate his command over this genre as well.

Sachin-da pioneered the practice of composing the tune first, with lyrics to be written befitting the metre of the tune. Later, Begum Akhtar was to go on record, saying, 'The "sur" of the singer should make the desired impact. Lyrics come later.' And much later, Gulzar too said that he considered the role of lyricists secondary to that of the composer. Sachin-da would sit with his lyricists to ensure that they wrote to the metre of his tune, at times even suggesting which words to use and which ones to avoid.

Singer Meena Kapoor whose first released song, '*Kisi se meri preet lagi*', was composed by Dada in *Aath Din* (1946), has said in an interview, that 'Sachin Kaka' used to focus on the phonetics. He would always like 'nice-sounding words'. 'For *Aath Din*, Sachin Kaka directed the lyricist to write phonetically pleasing words with his own examples. That is why I always feel his songs sound so sweet and pleasing.'

Lyricist Yogesh, who wrote for Dada in *Us Paar* (1974) and *Mili* (1974), told us that Dada had given him a tune to write the lyrics to. The next day, Dada Burman sat with a harmonium reading his lyrics written in Hindi, composing the song.

Being an accomplished singer himself, he could get the best out of any singer. His own singing, accompanied only by a harmonium, as a demonstration for rehearsing the singer, could upstage the final recording by the latter with full orchestra. Geeta Roy, Manna Dey, Hemant Kumar and Suman Kalyanpur, all had their first hit song with Dada. He also encouraged new singers like Kishore Kumar, Danny Denzongpa, his own son Pancham and Anuradha Paudwal to make their first forays in film music. Always game for the unconventional, Dada had both the brothers Raj Kapoor and Shammi Kapoor sing for themselves–Raj in *Dil Ki Rani* (1947) and Shammi in *Jeevan Jyoti* (1953).

Sachin-da's involvement in the depiction of his songs in the film used to be complete, perhaps next only to the director's. Dada would study the script, discuss the situation and offer suggestions even to accomplished directors. In *Sujata* and *Bandini*, he prevailed upon Bimal Roy to accept his approach, and in *Kala Bazar* it was Vijay Anand who accepted Dada's suggestion on how to shoot '*Rim jhim ke taraane leke aayi barsaat*'.

Vijay Anand considered Dada Burman the only 'visual' music composer who could comprehend the scene and create a suitable tune before even the lyrics were written. Once, Vijay Anand narrated to Dada that he wanted a song where the hero Dev Anand is shown walking as well as running. Dada created the tune of '*Khoya khoya chaand*' (*Kala Bazaar*, 1960), when the lyrics didn't even exist. No wonder then that composer-brothers Kalyanji-Anandji have said that when one hears a song composed by S.D. Burman, one is able to visualize the scene, and how it would have been picturized.

S.D. Burman's creativity continued to be at its peak right up to his last days. He was still in demand when he died in 1975, at the age of sixty-nine. In 1973, when SDB was sixty-seven years old, *Abhimaan* was released and went on to win him the Filmfare Award for best music. The other contenders, much younger than him, were Kalyanji-Anandji (*Zanjeer*), Laxmikant-Pyarelal (*Bobby* and *Daag*), and his own son R.D. Burman (*Yaadon Ki Baraat*). In comparison, most of his contemporaries, though much younger in age, had fallen silent for various reasons.

♫

During our interviews, several music directors openly admitted that some of their songs had been inspired from Dada's songs, even quoting particular songs. One music director even said that while composing folk songs, he kept in mind how Dada would have composed the song.

Kalyanji has gone on record to say that though all composers were good, if one has to rank them, he would rank S.D. Burman as the number one. Amitabh Bachchan called Dada Burman 'divine'. Composer S.N. Tripathi called him 'invincible' while praising his compositions. Gulzar sahib described Dada as 'The Prince of Indian Melody', while Pyarelal-ji said that if R.D. Burman was 'gold', S.D. Burman was a 'diamond'. Waheeda Rehman gushed, 'My most, most, most favourite music director. I just love him. I just love him. He was a sweetheart! Not only as a person, as a music director, absolutely great!'

Dada Burman was saintly in his behaviour, immersed in his music all day long, singing and creating tunes. He had no interest in gossip, politics or protests. Rarely attending meetings of the CMDA (Cine Music Directors Association), he would listen to their animated discussions about proposed increase in rates, royalties, copyrights, etc., with a smile, and quietly slip away after some time. CMDA's representative used to visit Dada to collect membership fees from him. Dada would drop the amount of the membership fees from his first-floor balcony.

Once, in the 1960s, some senior music directors expressed their displeasure when their songs were not featured in a popular weekly hit-parade. They sought a meeting and took their delegation to the sponsors' office to protest, after which the ranking system was discontinued for some time. Subsequently, in protest, the music directors concerned held their own 'Music Awards Night', where they criticized the weekly hit-parade selection and announced their own list of songs. Dada Burman was neither a part of the earlier delegation that visited the sponsors, nor a part of the subsequent 'Awards Night'.

If anything matched his passion for music, it was sports. He excelled in tennis at the college level, played football well, and later refereed football matches during his trips to Agartala. Whenever his favourite East Bengal team was in Bombay, he would stop all work to go and cheer for them at 'Cooperage' ground. He was so crazy about the game that one day he decided that all his musicians should play it. He ordered everyone to report to the Khar Gymkhana at six in the morning. He was the referee of course. The musicians went for ten days before they started making lame excuses and the numbers started dwindling.

He loved fishing and was a regular at Bombay's Powai Lake with Guru Dutt and Mukul Bose. He was often seen playing table tennis at 'Hotel Evergreen' in Khar, before moving to his bungalow, 'The Jet'. Dada was also a keen volleyball player but gave it up after he came to Bombay. He would encourage Gyan Mukherjee, Subodh Mukherjee, Ehsan (Saira Banu's father), Manna Dey and others to play a game of volleyball at the studio itself during breaks, and referee from outside. Manohari Singh once narrated how Dada Burman demonstrated his skills at a game of billiards at the 'Madras Club' to Madan Mohan who also happened to be there.

Once, he was seen seated enthusiastically on the front stone-bench during a hockey final at the stadium near Churchgate Station. Another time, he was the master conductor at a music night organized at the same stadium to raise funds for the Bombay Hockey Association. In his spare time at home, he used to play 'Patience', a game of cards.

♫

With the advent of the Internet, the thirst for learning more on Sachin-da revived. However, I realized soon enough that along with its benefits, the Internet came with a lot of undesirable, unreliable content. Without any research or authentication, such information was 'copy-pasted' by others, leading to myths being propagated all over. I joined fan groups dedicated to Sachin-da on Yahoo and Facebook. After my posts and anecdotes on the maestro were noticed, I was invited to be a co-owner/administrator for some of these groups.

Nearly five years ago, in mid-2009 to be exact, I decided to conduct my own research on S.D. Burman by meeting those who had worked with him and recording interviews. The interviews were limited to only those who had come in contact with Sachin-da directly, or those who knew someone who had interacted with him. We also interviewed a few who had studied SDB's music.

So far, we have conducted forty-six interviews in Mumbai, Pune, Kolkata and Agartala. Dada Burman, even after nearly forty years of his death, commands a lot of respect, love and reverence. Everyone we met was very happy to talk about Sachin-da, narrating anecdotes about the man, his simplicity, music, nature, personality, etc.

Initially, the interviews were voice recorded. Subsequently, wherever possible, we got the text printed and signed. Later, after acquiring a camcorder, the interviews were both video and voice recorded. In a couple of cases, the interviewee allowed only voice recording. All the material, so collected, has been handed over completely free to Sathya Saran and to the publishers because of my love for Sachin-da.

Much of what has been narrated and included in the book is based on or excerpted from these interviews. Together, they present a picture of a complex creator whose simple music continues to enthral us.

My quest is not complete – knowing Sachin-da, the man and the legend, would require far more than I can gather in a single lifetime.

♫

Besides thanking each and every one of our greats in the industry whom we have interviewed in the last five years, I take this opportunity to thank my friends who helped me in my mission.

Richa Lakhanpal, who accompanied me in almost all my interviews and without whose help it would have been impossible to complete this voluminous work. Jotting down important anecdotes as backup, asking pertinent questions, listening to and typing out the text which turned out to be the hardest part of the interviews, were some of the aspects where I had her support when I needed it most. I would also like to thank Richa's son Moksh, who was ever willing to help us with anything and everything electronic – transferring our videos, voice recordings, photographs, creating backups in hard disks / drop-box, etc.

Peeyush Sharma who, after shifting from Calcutta to Bangalore, became the founder secretary of 'Vintage Hindi Music Lovers Association'. The association used to organize live music performances and movie screenings and felicitated well-known music personalities, among other activities. He has several published articles to his credit, and a vast collection of songs, which was once even borrowed by HMV. He had conducted interviews with several cinema and music personalities, which had so far remained unpublished. Seven of his interviews are excerpted in this book, in addition to my own forty-plus interviews. He lives in Canada, from where he recently informed me that SDB is one of the two highest selling composers in Canada, RDB being the other one. This information is based on the data collected from music stores.

Mrinal Dev Burman, my friend, who has been very helpful during my trip to Agartala in 2011, making all the arrangements, including visits to important places connected with Sachin-da. I often call him early in the morning to wake him up and ask him for information on Sachin-da. He has helped translate text from Bangla to English and in innumerable other ways.

Mumbai
March 2014

Appendix

SHAKTI SAMANTA, on the music of *Aradhana*

I had decided that only Dada could make the music for this film. Only he could bring out the emotion I wanted, the way I wanted it. So I requested Dada. He listened to the story, and liked it immensely.

When it was time to record the songs, one song was urgently needed for the shoot to go on. Dada wanted to finish the recording for the song. This is where destiny comes in … each person comes with his own destiny… Dada wanted Rafi for the song. But Rafi sahab was on world tour at that time and would be out of India for a month. So, I requested Dada, 'Dada, Kishore has sung so many songs for you in so many films that have been made with Dev Anand. And Rajesh Khanna, being a new artiste has no established singing voice yet. Why don't we try recording the song with Kishore?'And Dada said, 'Okay, let us call Kishore.' Kishore sang and the recordings of 2-3 songs were completed, he sang very well. And Dada also agreed that my suggestion had been a good one. We felt almost unanimously that Kishore Kumar's voice matched Rajesh Khanna completely.

♫

HOMI MULLAN on S.D. Burman

(Interviewed by Moti Lalwani and Richa Lakhanpal on 28 April, 26 August, 13 September 2011)

How did you meet Sachin-da?

It was in 1963; I had gone and met RDB. Afterwards, RD took me to Dada Burman. Dada said, 'Is lambu ko kisne bulaya hai?' Pancham said, 'He plays certain instruments.' Dada said, 'Na, amaar kau re lagena, lagena.'

(No, I don't want anyone, don't want anyone.) Pancham requested Dada to hear me out. Dada tried me out and gave me a break. After that I started talking to him in Bengali. Dada was surprised, 'Tu Parsi hoke Bengali bolta hai, kaisa bolta hai?' I told him about my Calcutta background, and after he saw my skills he became friendlier.

Please tell us about Dada's team?

Dada's team consisted of all talented members like R.D. Burman, Basudev Chakraborti, Manohari Singh, Maruti Rao Keer, Bhupinder Singh, Bhanu Gupta, Devichand Chauhan, Amrut Rao, Chandrakant, Ranjeet Gazmer (Kancha), Sapan Chakravarty, Deepan Chatterji and Santosh (pet name Pheku, since he was jack of all trades, doing everything like background, timing, driving, etc.), and me. We all used to sit together to assist Dada.

During a break, Dada would ask us to have tea and snacks in such a way that we could not say yes! He would ask us, 'Tumi ekhhon khabe?', 'Tomra cha khabe?' Since we were in awe of him, our reply would be, 'Nahin, Dada nahin.' Naturally, Dada pooch rahe hain, toh hum kaise haan bolenge (*laughs*). He would always ask, instead of offering! (*guffaws*)

Dada Burman treated us like a family. He would practice. He would say, 'Main break loonga, toh ye log break lenge. Main chai peeyunga toh yeh log chai peeyinge. Main khana khaaunga, toh yeh log bhi khayenge. Aaj yeh log hain toh main hoon, main hoon toh yeh log hain.'

Dada Burman was very prompt and fair in payment to his musicians. In his financial dealings, Dada was very straightforward. Even if we had not played for a particular song, we would still get paid for it. Yes, as a sitting member of the group, we were getting paid, our complete fees including overtime and all other charges.

Did he accept suggestions?

He would accept suggestions whenever he thought they suited the situation and the tune. Otherwise, he would be rigid about making any changes. Once during a rehearsal—I don't remember for which song—we all were sitting together and suggesting, 'Dada, we will do like this, we will arrange it this way,' suggesting modernization of some sort. We continued, trying to convince him, 'Dada, if we were to do introduce this, it would sound better.' He got annoyed and left the harmonium, saying, 'Tum log karo, tum logon ko jo karna hai karo. Mere ko nahin karna hai! Amaar bhalo lage na!' (You all do it, do whatever you want to. I don't want to do it! I don't like it!) He stormed out of the room, adding, 'What I wanted, I have already done. I don't want such modernization. I don't want suggestions from any of you.' He walked out. Someone had to go out to bring him back. He kept on saying, 'Na, amaar kauke chai na, kauke na' (No, I don't want anyone, don't want anyone.) in Bengali, repeating it all the time.

What made him angry?

He would get angry if someone would crack a joke or someone would laugh during work. He would walk off the session. He never used to say anything, but we would realize ki hum log ne aisa kiya toh chale gaye. One of us would go in to pacify him and get him back.

Would he ask the other person to leave?

No, never. He would get excited, leave the music room and go inside his house, to come back after five minutes. Sometimes we had to go in and fetch him. He might even come back on his own, and sometimes, his wife would tell him, 'Korta, bachche hain' (After all they are like your children).

What were his other passions apart from music?

Burman Dada was fond of sports. Every morning, he also enjoyed playing 'Patience'. He was very fond of football. I remember an incident when I was living in Princess Street. He was a staunch supporter of East Bengal, while his wife supported Mohun Bagan. Whenever both the teams came to Bombay, Dada would come in his car to Princess Street. Being from Calcutta, naturally, I too was fond of football. Dada used to take me along, and I would sit with him and the other members at The Cooperage. We used to run into the comedian Agha quite often. Dada and Agha were on friendly terms. Both used to have fun at each other's expense. Whenever East Bengal would lose, Agha would tease Dada, 'Dada, aaj machi ka bhav kam ho gaya' (Dada, today the price of fish has fallen).

One day, it so happened that the East Bengal team lost. After the match, we came and sat in the car. As Dada was very quiet, no one spoke. The driver drove straight to his bungalow. Suddenly, Dada realized that I had not been dropped off at Princess Street. 'Tum idhar aake kya kar raha hai? Jaa, ghar jaa!' Dada exclaimed! Dada had brought me right up to his Khar bungalow to say, 'Go home. Tere ko kaun bulaya?' Dada was lost in his own thoughts and realized later that I was with him. Yes, he was in his own thoughts. Because, when he would go home, his wife, being a Mohun Bagan supporter, would ask, 'Korta, aaj kya hua?' (Karta, what happened today?) Dada didn't want me to hear about Meera Devi's comments on Mohun Bagan's victory, or East Bengal's loss. (*Homi can't stop laughing and repeats*), 'Tum idhar aake kya kar raha hai? Kyun aaya? Jao wapas jao!' (What are you doing here? Why have you come? Go, go back!) So, I had to take a train from Khar, and go all the way back to Marine Lines.

Did he have a sense of humour?

He did have a lot of humour. Bahut (*Starts giggling*), bahut hi tha! Besides, his style of speaking a mix of Bengali and Hindi was very humorous. Dada used to call me lambu, even though he himself was quite tall, some 6 feet or so. He would often say, 'Lambu ko bulake lao'.

Once, during the making of *Talash* (1969), O.P. Ralhan had to shoot a cabaret. He came and described the situation. Gesturing with his hands, he said, 'Dada, hundred girls will come like this and dance like this, hundred girls will come like this and they will do like this.'

Then, when the picturisation took place, there was only Helen and just a few girls. So, Dada asked, 'OP, where are those hundred girls you promised?' He would tease even the producers. It was '*Karle pyar karle*...' (*Sings a few lines of the song.*) It's my favourite song, I like it. See, how I remembered it!

How was he as a person?

There was a childlike innocence about him. We had gone for the premier of Shankar-Jaikishan's film *Suraj* (1966). Dada Burman was invited, so he asked me to come along, saying, 'You meet me at Liberty Cinema.' In those days, Liberty Cinema was one of the top cinema halls. Shankarji was sitting in the front row along with Sharda and other invitees. Dada and I were sitting two-three rows from the last row. From the time we came in, Dada sat like this. (Homi lifts up his legs, keeping his feet up on the chair.) Paon upar karke (He sat with his feet up), aur screen par woh gana laga (and on the screen that song played). (Homi is unable to control his laughter.)

'*Titli udi*' sung by Sharda?

Yes, and Dada asked me loudly, 'Who is singing this song?' And, Shankarji turned around to stare at me. But Dada, oblivious to Shankarji's stares, continued, 'Kitna naak se gaa rahi hai woh!' Some people turned around to look at us.

Selective in signing movies

He was asked to score music for a film. Dada used to hear the story first, before signing the picture. I was present there. All of us were present listening to the story. It was in 1974. I am giving you a first-hand account of this incident. He heard the story for some time. It turned out to be a mythological. He got up and said, 'Why have you brought this story to me? Take it to Chitragupta, or some other music director. Any other music director will do a better job than me. Give me a picture which requires folk, classical or romantic music.' Nowadays, if someone goes to a music director, he will say, 'Yes, yes, forget the picture, I'll create songs that you will be very happy.' Homi starts laughing.

On the music of *Aradhana* (1969)

All the songs of *Aradhana* have been created by Burman Dada.

All the songs of Kishore too are by Dada?

Yes, all songs. Dada used to do everything. Pancham-da used to assist him. Basu, Manohariji and Maruti Rao were his other three assistants. In the song "*Mere sapnon ki rani*" a Jeep is being driven by actor Sujit Kumar following a moving train. During the picturisation of the song, Sujit Kumar is shown playing the mouthorgan, which is the music in the mukhda. But in antaras, wherever Sujit Kumar has been shown playing mouthorgan, Dada Burman had used the guitar. So, Dada Burman reacted, 'What is this? Guitar's music is played and you are showing mouth organ!' Dada was quite annoyed about it.

Did Dada mention it to Shakti Samanta?

Yes. During the trial, Dada told Shakti Samanta, 'I have given the music of guitar, and you have shown the mouthorgan being played!' I was present there. Dada got upset. You would have seen the song. Watch it on YouTube again. You'll realize that in antaras, whenever mouthorgan is being played on screen, you hear music of guitar!

Then there is *'Roop tera mastana'*. There is a specialty about this song, please write it down, Dada has created such an evergreen song, that it is popular even now. Today's youngsters who are college going students, they too listen till date and enjoy it. (Starts humming the tune.) In this song, all important instruments have been used: saxophone, accordion, vibraphone, duggi. Sax is played by Manohariji, accordion by Kersi Lord, vibraphone by Buji Lord and duggi by me. In the stanzas, claves have been used. Tuk, tuk, tuk, that has been played by Chandrakant Naik, known as stick in the film industry.

(Sings 'Gunguna rahe hain bhanwre, khil rahi hai kali kali, gali gali, kali kali'.) That was Dada! Dada beautified the entire song by introducing scaling. That's why this song became a hit! The high point of the song is the 'bridge', which contributes towards its success.

Bridge meaning?

The tempo changes from slow to fast in 'Gunguna rahen hain bhanwre, khil rahi hai kali kali, gali gali, kali kali'. What has been sung as 'kali kali, gali gali' has made the song outstanding. Dada had created the meter for the song. It is very difficult to write in that meter, but the lyricist Anand Bakshi did a very good job, and Dada was satisfied.

♫

STORY BEHIND SOME OF THE OTHER SONGS

'O panchhi pyaare': *Bandini* (1963)

This beautiful song sung by Asha Bhonsle was to be picturised on women undergoing their term in prison. During the song they are shown engaged in manual cleaning and grinding of the grain. This was to be shown with the aid of 'supra', which is supposed to make a particular sound, while the grain is being separated from the loose husk. Dada Burman thought of a very novel idea to create the sound the supra makes while cleaning the grain. As suggested by him, we used wheat and rice mixed together and the mix was rolled from side to side in the supra. On YouTube you see the video and hear the sound which exactly matches the sound of supra cleaning the grain.

'Aaj ko junely raat maa': *Talash* (1969)
These words were introduced by Santosh Singh, that's why he was known as 'Jack of all trades!' He was nicknamed 'Pheku'. He was from Nepal and 'Junely raat' words are Nepalese meaning 'moonlit night'.

For all the movies that you worked with him, right from 1963 till his last, did Dada create the music entirely on his own?
Yes, by him only.

That's definite, that the music is made by him. It is not made by…, his three assistants, or…?
No, no, no.

… R.D. Burman?
No, no, not at all.

But some RDB fans claim otherwise?
You have to overlook that. Dada would sometimes take advice from us, but he would follow only if thinks it suits, otherwise no. Dada Burman was the captain of the ship, with RDB as a commander under him. The three main assistants, Basudev Chakraborti, Manohari Singh and Maruti Rao Keer were like his lieutenant commanders, and the rest of us Devichand, Ranjit Gazmer, Amrut Rao, Chandrakant Naik, Bhanu Gupta and I were sitting members of his team. Should the captain order to turn right, we will have to go towards right. Even if you want to go to the left, you will have to veer towards the right. You have to follow the captain of the ship!

♫

SOME SNIPPETS

Learning Marathi

Once what happened, Dada decided to learn some Marathi. He asked Amrut Rao Katkar to teach him. The first word that Amrut Rao tried to teach him was jhevla (will you eat?). Dada, being from the north-east, pronounced it in a way making it sound like an abusive word in Marathi. Meera Devi, who was fluent in Marathi, heard it from inside and summoned Dada. Those present could hear her saying, 'Korta, don't say that. Don't learn otherwise.' That was his first and last session of learning Marathi! Amrut Rao would be able to tell you more about it.

On Sachin-da's socializing
If ever Dada went to a party, he would take about half a peg of whiskey and fill up the rest with water or soda. Sometimes, he might take a glass of wine. He would circulate amongst other guests. Dada would never drink more than that. Haan, about Pancham-da you may say, but not our Dada.

♫

USTAAD RAIS KHAN on S.D. Burman

Which music directors have you worked with in the film industry?
Ask me who I have not worked with. I have worked with all the greats, they were all giants.

What can you share about S.D. Burman?
I did not work with him. I do not know much about him. But once when I was going past his house, someone said that Burman Sahab lives here, would you like to meet him? I replied, 'Yes, why not.' I went along. He was sitting in his customary white dhoti-kurta. There were three doors leading from the hall, all behind him. Then something funny happened. It is a good story.

I noticed Pancham standing behind Dada and signalling me, tell him you want tea. At first I did not understand. I kept staring at Pancham. (*Copies Pancham, 'Ask for tea'*.) Finally, I understood. I told Dada, 'Dada, hum chai peeyenge.' And Dada responded, 'What are you saying? Tea? Arre Baba, you are such a young boy and you are asking for tea! Kids don't drink tea, do they?' Then he added, 'There is no milk.' But by then Pancham entered, with cups of tea. Dada says, 'Arre, why have you got so much tea!' (*We all have a good laugh.*)

After tea, he decided to have a paan. He was sorting the leaves very carefully as if they were rationed, and I could see that Pancham was signalling and winking at me again. I understood the signal. He wanted me to ask for a paan. So I said, 'What a nice fragrance, can you share some of the paan with me too?' Dada said: ' You eat paan? Such a young boy? Chee-chee-chee! It is very bad', (*giggles*) and he did not give me any paan. And Pancham was laughing away in the other room.

♬

ANANDJI BHAI on S.D. Burman

(Anandji is one half of the well-known composer duo Kalyanji-Anandji)

He was very close to Kalyanji bhai?

Yes very close, we were like his own. He would eat paan, which was a habit with me too. When we would be travelling outstation, and if we did not send paan leaves to his room, he would get upset. He would phone and ask, why has your paan not come yet, why have you not sent it. So Kalyanji would say, 'Yes, yes, sorry, I am sending it right away.' The trouble was, he would wake up early, long before we did. He also loved Sindhi papad a lot. He would call, 'You have forgotten me, you've not sent me any papad, you don't care about me.' It was like he was a member of our family, or we of his, he would talk to us with the same familiarity and freedom.

Tell us about his music, his songs.

He would always check the situation to see if it was good enough to make the song popular. He would tell the director, 'I will give this song for this situation, I will not change it.' If the director demurred, he would tell him, 'You have no brains, you don't know anything.' All the directors knew how straightforward he was. He would tell them straight off. He also took on limited work. He would do two films in a year, if someone came to him with a third, he would tell him, 'Don't you have brains? I am already working on two films. I will not do anything else this year. Come to me next year.' It showed he was not greedy for more money, which more work would surely get him.

♬

ANECDOTES by Archisman Mozumdar, a fan of SDB and RDB

On a flight to Kolkata from Mumbai in 2005, I had the good fortune to be seated beside the great singer-composer, Bhupen Hazarika. As the flight was about to land, I mustered enough courage to greet him. As the discussion gathered momentum, I asked him about a song by Manna Dey in the film *Aarop* (1973) which was composed by him. The song, '*Haath mere hai madhu ka pyaala*' was beautifully rendered by Manna Dey (singing for the actor Vinod Mehra). The antara of this song was very similar to the antara of S.D. Burman's '*Premer shamaadhi teere*'. Dr Hazarika looked at me with a benign smile and said, 'When one spends his lifetime in the north-east, it is difficult not to come under the influence of Karta and his songs'. '*Premer shamaadhi teere*' is arguably SD's most celebrated Bengali song and was a massive hit. Tuned by his dear friend, Himangshu Dutta, Karta sang it with an emotional fervour that unerringly touched the listeners' hearts. A measure of how popular the song was is illustrated in this anecdote:

*

In the mid 1960s, Mohun Bagan had won the Rovers Cup tournament that used to be held in Bombay at the Cooperage Football Ground. After the award ceremony, as the players were celebrating the victory, S.D. Burman came over to the dressing room to meet the players. S.D. Burman, as all know, was a die-hard fan of the rival club of Kolkata, East Bengal Football Club. Nevertheless, to show his admiration and solidarity to the players from Bengal, he turned up to meet them. The players were awestruck as S.D. Burman was a composing giant in Bombay by then. The celebrated captain of the Mohun Bagan team, Chuni Goswami, then requested the famous singer composer to render the incomparable song '*Premer shamaadhi teere*' (which was also known as '*Taj Mahal*' on the record labels). The great man duly obliged, and the players, officials, and bystanders had a memorable evening to cherish for the rest of their lifetime.

*

Vijay Anand is widely acknowledged as one of the finest in the industry in terms of positioning a song in a movie and its picturisation. He can be safely credited with some of the finest Navketan releases since the late 1950s. Vijay Anand has gone on record in an interview to say that S.D. Burman was very perceptive about the power and impact of the medium of films and took a keen interest in understanding the situation of a song and its context in the landscape of the entire movie. In the same interview, he has mentioned about a particular incident where it was S.D. Burman who had suggested that the song '*Rimjhim ke taraane le-ke aayi barsaat*' in *Kala Bazaar* (1960) be picturised on the hero and heroine with the song playing only in the background. Vijay Anand immediately liked the idea and thus was the lovely Rafi-Geeta duet created.

In my opinion, this song, with visuals of a rain-lashed promenade of South Bombay, the fleeting images of flashbacks and the muted yet expressive faces of the debonair hero Dev Anand and the dainty heroine Waheeda, is one of the best-picturised songs in the annals of Indian movies. It is as timeless as the Raj-Nargis duet from *Shri 420*, and S.D. Burman had suggested on how to picturise it.

♫

Excerpts from an interview with ANIL SARKAR, Minister, Higher Education, Information and Cultural Affairs, Government of Tripura
(Interview conducted by Moti Lalwani)

Tell us a few things about what the government is doing to popularize the music of S.D. Burman.
We had celebrated Sachin Karta's centenary year in 2006 throughout the state of Tripura by arranging programmes based on his music. Our government has plans to concentrate on Sachin Karta, our cultural heritage, who has brought the state of Tripura on the world map of music and culture. You see, West Bengal has Rabindranath Tagore, both West Bengal and Bangladesh have Kazi Nazrul Islam, Assam has Bhupen Hazarika and we have our own Sachin Karta to be proud of. Hence, as part of an ongoing process, we have made plans for the next ten years to popularize Sachin Karta and his school of music. This is our cultural commitment.

In ten years what do you intend to do, and how will you do that?
We intend to create awareness amongst the younger generation throughout the entire state that Sachin Karta belongs to us and we belong to Sachin Karta. He is our cultural heritage, and his songs and his style are our inheritance. Out of 40 community development blocks, 5 artists per block will be selected and trained on SDB's music. These artists will be selected through block-level competitions, and workshops will be arranged in each block.

Other than popularizing the Sachin school of music among the younger generation of Tripura, what do you think requires more emphasis to know about this maestro properly?
India knows him as S.D. Burman. Very few of the rest of India other than Bengali-speaking zones have knowledge about his basic ingredients and styles, which are from the soil of this area. If we can highlight those fields, automatically the rich heritage and folk culture of this region will be popularized. We are planning for some music concerts at Kolkata, Guwahati and some other places for this purpose.

Acknowledgements

Ideas come from many directions. And the idea for the form this book would take came from a book by Michael Ondaatje titled *Coming Through Slaughter*. If it was not for Ranjit Panchal who lent me the book, (and never asked for it back), this book might have read differently.

For supporting the fantasy that a biography can be written in the form of a mosaic, and letting me discuss it obsessively over a series of coffee house meetings, a sincere thanks to my editor, Shantanu Ray Chaudhuri. A word of thanks also to Prerna Gill for her very pertinent and helpful suggestions on the text.

To Moti Lalwani, I owe thanks for all the legwork I was saved by his conducting relevant interviews on my behalf, and for handing me his files of clippings.

To Karthika, publisher and friend, thank you for your continued trust in my writing.

And a big hug to my entire family for letting me write whenever I had to, and not making me feel guilty about being absent though present. That is a rare gift to receive.

About the Author

Best known for her long association with *Femina*, which she edited for twelve years, Sathya Saran is the author of a book of short stories – *The Dark Side* – apart from the critically acclaimed biographies, *Years with Guru Dutt: Abrar Alvi's Journey*, *Baat Niklegi toh Phir: The Life* and *Music of Jagjit Singh* and *Hariprasad Chaurasia: Breath of Gold.*

Passionate about writing, Sathya conceptualised and curates an offbeat writers' conclave titled 'The Spaces between Words: The Unfestival', held in Vijaynagar (Karnaṭaka) and Ratnagiri (Maharashtra), India.